IN THE SHADOW
OF STATUES

IN THE SHADOW OF STATUES

A White Southerner Confronts History

MITCH LANDRIEU

VIKING

VIKING

An imprint of Penguin Random House LLC

375 Hudson Street

New York, New York 10014

penguin.com

ISBN 9780525559443 (hardcover)
ISBN 9780525559450 (ebook)

Printed in the United States of America
1 3 5 7 9 10 8 6 4 2

Set in Bembo MTPro
Designed by Amy Hill

Penguin is committed to publishing works of quality and
integrity. In that spirit, we are proud to offer this book to our
readers; however, the story, the experiences, and the words
are the author's alone.

CONTENTS

For my incredible wife, Cheryl, and our wonderful children:
Grace, Emily, Matt, Ben, and Will

Thank you. I love you all so much.

IN THE SHADOW
OF STATUES

Can Someone Get Me a Crane?

Here I was, mayor of a major American city in the midst of a building boom like no other, filled with million-dollar construction jobs, and I couldn't find anyone in town who would rent me a crane. Are you kidding me?!

For the last eight years, we'd experienced the most aggressive rebuilding phase in our city's history. We'd benefited from nearly $8 billion in public and private-sector investments, from housing to hospitals to new retail stores to streets. We'd awarded billions of dollars of construction work to private contractors to actually do the rebuilding, and there are cranes across the skyline. Many of the construction companies, large and small, have made record profits during my time in City Hall.

The people of the city of New Orleans, through their elected government, had made the decision to take down four Confederate monuments, and it wasn't sitting well with some of the powerful business interests in the state. When I put out a bid for contractors to take them down, a few responded. But they were immediately attacked on social media, got threatening calls at work and at home, and were, in general, harassed. This kind of thing normally never happens. Afraid, most naturally backed away. One contractor stayed with us. And then his car was firebombed. From that moment on, I couldn't find anyone willing to take the statues down.

I tried aggressive, personal appeals. I did whatever I could. I personally drove around the city and took pictures of the countless cranes and crane companies working on dozens of active construction projects across New Orleans. My staff called every construction company and every project foreman. We were blacklisted. Opponents sent a strong message that any company that dared step forward to help the city would pay a price economically and even personally.

Can you imagine? In the second decade of the twenty-first century, tactics as old as burning crosses or social exclusion, just dressed up a little bit, were being used to stop what was now an official act authorized by the government in the legislative, judicial, and executive branches.

This is the very definition of institutionalized racism. You may have the law on your side, but if someone else controls the money, the machines, or the hardware you need to make your new law work, you are screwed. I learned more and more that this is exactly what has happened to African Americans over the last three centuries. This is the difference between de jure and de facto discrimination in today's world. You can finally win legally, but still be completely unable to get the job done. The picture painted by African Americans of institutional racism is real and was acting itself out on the streets of New Orleans during this process in real time.

In the end, we got a crane. Even then, opponents at one

point had found their way to one of our machines and poured sand in the gas tank. Other protesters flew drones at the contractors to thwart their work. But we kept plodding through. We were successful, but only because we took extraordinary security measures to safeguard equipment and workers, and we agreed to conceal their identities. It shouldn't have to be that way.

What follows is my account of the tumultuous events that led to the crisis over taking down the figures of Robert E. Lee, Jefferson Davis, and Pierre Gustave Toutant Beauregard and a monument honoring the White League, a Reconstruction-era organization of racial militants.

Learning the story of these structures, why they were built and by whom, made clear to me, probably for the first time in my life, the lens through which many, though certainly not all, Southerners have seen our regional identity since the Civil War. The statues were not honoring history, or heroes. They were created as political weapons, part of an effort to hide the truth, which is that the Confederacy was on the wrong side of humanity. They helped distort history, putting forth a myth of Southern chivalry, the gallant "Lost Cause," to distract from the terror tactics that deprived African Americans of fundamental rights from the Reconstruction years through Jim Crow until the civil rights movement and the federal court decisions of the 1960s. Institutional inequities in the economic, education, criminal justice, and housing systems exist to this very day.

I am well aware of the emotional investment of many Southerners whose ancestors fought in the Civil War, of the popular interest in historical events, of how families lost loved ones, came through, and coped. I do not mean dishonor to these people. My concern is with the political meaning of the monuments in New Orleans, who put them there, and why: the perversion of history.

The statues were symbols. Symbols matter. We use them in telling the stories of our past and who we are, and we choose them carefully. Once I learned the real history of these statues, I knew there was only one path forward, and that meant making straight what was crooked, making right what was wrong. It starts with telling the truth about the past.

Race—the word, its many meanings, the constellation of "issues" that the word connotes—does something to the human eye. Sometimes, it's hot and uncomfortable when you are around people who can only see color. People of color become objects, or problems, not humans. It's often these same people who, when asked about history, insist to themselves and us that they are not at fault, that history happened before them, that it's time to move on—in fact, it was all so far back it might as well never have happened. Or they grasp one convenient piece of history, say, the rightful place of Confederate statues, a reminder of why Southern soldiers fought and died. But that is not the whole story of what these statues mean and *why* they were erected.

And the misuse of history is inflamed by the anger burning through demonstrations today, anger fueled by white supremacists and neo-Nazis who have stolen the meaning of Southern heritage from many whites who abhor their ideology but still hold hard to a rose-colored nostalgia for the past. It is a view of history that I, respectfully, do not share; but I understand where they are coming from, and why many people feel as they do. Faulkner famously wrote, "The past is never dead; it's not even past." We live those words today, all too painfully.

Race is America's most traumatic issue, one that we have

not nearly worked through. The true measure of a great country is the quality of justice it affords to all. Dr. Martin Luther King, Jr., insisted, "True peace . . . is the presence of justice." It is a long, rugged road for all people to find that peace, and our job is to stay on that path, even as we make progress.

This book also follows my personal story. As I look back at key passages in my life, I think about the racial realities that shadowed me from an early age and the remarkable influence of my parents, Moon and Verna Landrieu, in fostering an ethos of honesty and fair play toward all people in my eight siblings and me. Race percolates through so many of the major events in New Orleans, including most recently the career of David Duke and the path of Hurricane Katrina through our city, and so those episodes are part of this story, too.

These last eight years have given me the wonderful privilege of serving as mayor of the city where I was born and raised. New Orleans is a town with a song in its heart and a swing in its step. We also have a history of racial injustice that we must never stop confronting in order to build a stronger and more equitable city for all who call it home. Everyone alive today has inherited this country's difficult history. Although in recent years we celebrated the fiftieth anniversary of the March on Washington and elected an African American president twice, the big message we should hear from the streets of Baltimore and Ferguson and Charlottesville and New Orleans is that we are not done; we have more work to do.

A house divided against itself cannot stand, but to heal our divisions we must be able to hear one another, see one another, understand one another and feel one another. Once we start to listen rather than speak, see rather than look away, we will realize a simple truth: we are all the same. We all want the same thing—peace, prosperity, and economic opportunity. And for our kids to have a better life than we do. There are many who are cynical and believe we cannot change, that our divisions are somehow part of the natural order of things. This is the moment to prove them wrong.

This has been a long and personal story for me. I hope that this book meets each reader wherever they are in their own journey on race, and that my own story gives each reader the courage to continue to move forward. I hope that this book helps create hope for a limitless future. Now is the time to actually make this city and country the way they always should have been. Now is the time for choosing our path forward.

CHAPTER 1

Broadmoor

Your daddy ruined the city."

I was thirteen when the woman yelled those words at me, a newly minted eighth grader at Jesuit High School, where my father had been a star athlete a quarter century before. Earlier that day, Father Harry Tompson, the principal, a jovial man but quite the disciplinarian, summoned me to his office. "There has been a threat made against your life," he said gravely. Someone had called the switchboard with an alarming message. With a wary eye, Father Tompson escorted me across Banks Street to the gym, letting me go in for basketball practice early.

It was 1973, and three years since my father, Moon Landrieu, was inaugurated as mayor of New Orleans. He had spent those years fulfilling campaign promises to give African Americans access to public contracts and jobs in city government, while prodding hotels and restaurants to do more than simply welcome black customers—that is, to hire black people above the level of dishwashers, maids, and bellhops. Segregation practices were eroding after federal court decisions, which angered and frightened many whites, who feared the political power of newly registered African American voters in a city that was still at that point 65 percent white. New Orleans might have been among the crown jewels of the South, but with white flight to the suburbs, the demographics, power structures, and economy were changing quickly. Today the city is 60 percent black.

My father was a pragmatist, and a pro-business New Deal–style Democrat. He was also morally grounded. The credo he stressed to my siblings and me was simple, if profound: "Be honest, and be fair."

Growing up, I was vaguely aware of my dad taking heat over politics, but when he sat down for dinner with us, which he did nearly every night, he didn't mention rabble-rousers who jeered at City Council meetings. We had free-flowing conversations, warm with humor, as he asked about us, our lives, what we did that day. We often had guests in those years, too. But a backlash was building, and about to catch me.

That day at practice, I joked about the death threat as guys came into the locker room; everyone thought it was cool. A few minutes later, one of my friends ran in and said, "There's some lady outside calling your name, cursing you, *saying she wants to kill you.*" We did the only thing that teenage boys would do—go outside and see the threat. From the cement platform above the field-house steps, I recognized her right away, an older woman who had a fiery presence in local politics. I had seen her on TV news in the late sixties, protesting when my father was a councilman-at-large and they took down the Confederate flag in the City Council chambers. She kept on protesting after that. As I stood there, she began yelling profanities. "You got black blood!" she finally snarled. "That explains it all!"

My friends were riveted. She stuck a hand into her purse. Someone yelled, "She has a gun!" They all scattered, leaving me to face what was to come. I had a shaky sense that she wouldn't shoot an unarmed Jesuit prefreshman in cold blood. She pulled out a business card with her name, wrote on it "Your father is a nigger lover," and threw it at me. "He is sending this city to hell!" she shouted. Then she bolted off.

I was in a churn of confusion, but what I felt more than anything was pity. I didn't think that she would hurt me; I could tell that she was challenged, not in full control—that in some awful way she was crippled by her beliefs. That night I told my father what had happened. "She's harmless," he said. I knew he had been dealing with people like her for some time; his optimism and upbeat politics registered on me in a calm, steady way. That encounter at school marked the first time I felt the hater's pain, the frustration and fury spilling out at things beyond her control. I have seen this expression of spirit throughout my life since then. Art and music engage the human heart and transcend time; sadly, so does hatred. I learned this one early.

When I announced in 2015 that we were going to take down four icons of the Confederate past, the front desk at City Hall logged a flood of calls from people burning with anger. The familiar hate was back.

"He's ruining this city, just like his father. He's gonna pay!"

"He better watch out!"

And yet, other voices from the past came back to comfort me.

"Say, baby, how's your daddy? Best mayor we had."

"Hey, young man! Tell your momma hello! Love that woman."

I cannot remember a time when the issue of race was not part of my life or our family's. It's like a song that you cannot get out of your head; it keeps playing over and over. Race is a soundtrack that stays with me. New voices roll in: hostility at one side; a benevolent approval—love, if you will—at the other; and a swirl of voices in the middle range, hashing out what it means to be American, our common identity as citizens. I take heart that many white people have traveled far in their views on race. Many young people embrace diversity as a natural order of things, with no memory of a South governed by segregationists and white supremacists. And yet, today's public square teems with hatred of an intensity we haven't seen since the 1960s. The violence by white nationalists in Charlottesville, Virginia, shows that hatred will grow if we do not shine the light of God's love and human reason on the darkness and chart a path of healing for the country as a whole.

New Orleans mirrors a map of the world, a city where people of many countries have settled, shaping a beloved culture that has been enriched with jazz, Creole and Cajun cuisine, and so much more. We've shared culture across racial lines, but we also have played a seminal role in some of the saddest chapters in American history. More humans were sold into slavery in New Orleans than anywhere else in the country. Hundreds of thousands of souls were sold here, then shipped up the Mississippi River to lives of forced labor, of misery, of rape, of torture. As we entertain visitors from around the world along our beautiful riverfront, it is hard to fathom that at this very spot, ships emptied their human cargo from Senegal, marching their captives down the street to what is now one of our famous hotels, but there are no historical markers on that path. No monuments or flags to the lives destroyed.

New Orleans is where black Creoles launched a legal challenge to segregated public transportation, a case that led to the 1896 Supreme Court decision *Plessy v. Ferguson*, which enshrined Jim Crow's "separate but equal" into law. In 1892 a mixed-race man named Homer Plessy attempted to board a whites-only train car but was arrested because he was one-eighth black. Sixty years later, Freedom Riders coming to New Orleans were beaten to a bloody pulp. Today, though, even as white identity politics rage, I take comfort that my city understands that diversity is our strength, greeting visitors with warmth and a cultural effervescence, even as we resolve to work hard to evolve and heal. We all have so far to go.

I'm struck by how often people describe others first by the color of their skin—black people, African Americans, people of color. When I think about the people I love and have learned from, I don't think about their color; I remember their words. My family set me on a path, but many others helped guide me.

"The most important thing to remember is that no one can take away from you anything that you learn," Norman Francis told me when I was just a boy. Dr. Francis served forty-seven years as president of Xavier, the historically black Catholic university in New Orleans. He was one of the first two African American students at Loyola University New Orleans law school in the 1950s, where he and my father met and forged their lifelong friendship. Dr. Francis received a Presidential Medal of Freedom from President George W. Bush for his work in rebuilding Xavier after Hurricane Katrina. "The future belongs to those who are educated," Norman often said in his calm, comforting way.

Other voices echoed that woman's on the steps of the Jesuit gym.

"Moon the Coon!" barked a man when I picked up the phone as a kid, long before caller ID. The man hung up. I have no clear memory of my father talking about the hate calls we got; maybe I've blotted it all out, because the more vivid, lasting memory of my adolescence is jumping into the car with my dad on Saturdays as he drove around the city, visiting playgrounds, police stations, fire stations, and city work sites. The city was in his bloodstream, as it is in mine.

Maurice Edwin Landrieu was born in 1930, the younger of two brothers. They grew up on Adams Street, a working-class neighborhood in the Uptown area. The house was twelve feet wide and fifty feet deep and faced a graveyard. Dad slept with his brother, Joe, in the storage room of a storefront grocery run by my grandma, Loretta Landrieu. My grandpa, Joseph Geoffrey Landrieu, had a third-grade education and worked for the public utility company, then called NOPSI, in one of the power stations. I remember him tenderly; Grandpa Landrieu died when I was seven.

The nickname "Moon" was apparently given to Dad from Uncle Joe early on, that's all we know. Everyone called him Moon, even in college, law school, and after he established his law practice and got into politics; in 1969 he had his first name legally changed to Moon.

My father, Uncle Joe, and their parents would by any definition have been classified as working-class poor, but from everything Dad has told me, his childhood was happy. He never knew or felt that he was poor. Miraculously, my grandparents steered both sons to Jesuit, the leading Catholic high school for boys. Dad entered Loyola University in 1948 on a baseball scholarship, where he met Father Louis J. Twomey, S.J., an important mentor. Father Twomey was an adviser to labor unions, and in lectures on ethics at the law school, insisted that racial segregation was morally wrong. This was the earliest stirring of the civil rights movement in New Orleans. Father Twomey hosted organizational meetings for early civil rights activists. In the 1950s he published a mimeographed newsletter, "Christ's Blueprint for the South," which was years ahead of Southern elected officials in advocating for greater social justice for African Americans.

The other pivotal person from those years in Dad's life was the woman he would marry. My mother, born Verna Satterlee, met my father in the 1950s when they were undergraduates at Loyola. Verna was one of seven children born to Kent Satterlee and Olga Macheca. Unlike my dad's family, the Satterlees were comfortably middle class; my mother was born on the corner of South Prieur Street and General Pershing, just across the street from the house where she would live most of her life. She had uncommon energy, nerves of steel, and a heart filled with a servant's spirit. She had gone to Loyola after high school at Ursuline Academy, the same high school all five of my sisters and both of my daughters would attend through middle school.

When people ask me where my father got his progressive views on race, it takes a while to explain how the convergence of these people—Father Twomey, Verna Satterlee, and Norman Francis—changed Dad's idea of race relations. My parents were both serious young Catholics. In 1956 Archbishop Joseph Rummel announced that New Orleans parochial schools would enroll black children—a controversial move that brought white protesters outside the Church offices (it took till 1962 to desegregate the schools). Committed to Rummel's policy no matter how long it took, Twomey was a driven Jesuit on the right side of history. And Norman Francis, with his polite tenacity, opened my father's heart and mind; their friendship sealed Dad's conviction that segregation laws were morally unjust and economically unfair. He knew that Norman was every bit as good as himself, but because of his color he had been denied the benefits that Dad had had every step of the way. They were tough, courageous, honest, and fairminded men. But above all else, they were just friends.

Dad graduated from Loyola two years ahead of Mom. He entered Loyola law school on an army scholarship that committed him to service as a military lawyer after graduation. Mom took another route. She entered an Ursuline convent to train for the life of a nun. But God had other plans for her. She left the convent; they married in 1954, at just about the time Dad's friend Norman married Blanche Macdonald. The Francises had six children; we all grew up together, the Francis kids a daily reminder that the racist things some of our white friends said about black people were untrue according to what my eyes had seen and my ears had heard. The ties we had with the Francis family—and other black families as my dad got deeper into politics—shaped my family's rejection of the racial mentality of the Old South. My dad today also insists he was being somewhat selfish— because Norman was and is his best friend, the stances he took were often to benefit himself.

After Dad finished law school, my parents moved to Arlington, Virginia, where the young lawyer worked in the Judge Advocate General's Corps at the Pentagon. Their first child, Mary Loretta, was born there in 1955. They moved back to

New Orleans in the late fifties; Dad began practicing law and raising kids. The idea of electoral office was quite a leap for an attorney approaching thirty, with four young children and a fifth (yours truly) on the way; he won a seat in the legislature in 1959 with the support of the reform mayor deLesseps Story "Chep" Morrison.

Louisiana's governor at the time was Jimmie Davis, a country-western entertainer famous for his song "You Are My Sunshine." He had served a term as governor in the 1940s and made a comeback as an avowed segregationist in 1959, at a time when the Louisiana legislature was purging African Americans from the voting rolls. Southern white resistance was growing against the Supreme Court's 1954 *Brown v. Board of Education* ruling that racial segregation in schools was unconstitutional. In Baton Rouge, the legislature in 1960 pushed laws to thwart desegregation of the schools, which under federal law would soon begin in New Orleans. Governors like Orval Faubus in Arkansas, Ross Barnett in Mississippi, and George Wallace in Alabama all used ruses like this along with fearmongering tactics to keep African Americans out of white schools and colleges. The racial demagoguery triggered violent behavior; two men died in the 1962 riot at the University of Mississippi sparked by the registration of James Meredith, the first African American student to attend the school.

My father voted against twenty-nine Jim Crow laws in the legislature in 1960. He was serving his black and white constituents, and in such a volatile environment the stance he took showed real courage, as one of only two dissenting white votes. One evening, my father got on the elevator in the hotel where he was staying in Baton Rouge, only to confront State Senator Willie Rainach, a hard-edged racist, and Leander Perez, the district attorney of Plaquemines Parish, an area of plantations, citrus groves, fisheries, and marshland south of New Orleans. *Demagogue* is too soft a term to describe Perez, a long-standing member of the state's all-white Citizens Council, a buttoned-down version of the Ku Klux Klan. He was Louisiana's George Wallace and ran his political fiefdom with a prison stay waiting for any demonstrators. Though no one knew it at the time, he was also swindling the parish government out of a fortune in mineral leases on public land he controlled. Several years after Perez died, the parish government filed suit and forced the Perez heirs to relinquish sixty thousand acres of land and pay $10 million in back royalties.

Perez and Willie Rainach surrounded my father in the elevator.

"We know your kind," said Rainach, jabbing a forefinger in Dad's chest. *"We're going to get you!* You're done!"

I was in my mother's womb at that moment when my father's life was threatened, and was born later that summer, on August 16, 1960. The fifth of nine children. Right in the middle. I have been in the middle of a journey on race ever since. There has not been a moment in my life when we haven't been tackling these issues personally or politically.

My father was a marked man to the racist right; but in standing up for his values, he earned the respect of black people in his district, as well as a good measure of whites, who though unsure about desegregation, saw him as a leader willing to make hard decisions and with the courage to speak the truth. A few years later he won a City Council seat even though New Orleans had a strong white voting majority. There he and Council members Philip Ciaccio and Eddie Sapir spearheaded the removal of the Confederate flag that was still on display in public chambers.

Leander Perez, meanwhile, had orchestrated Governor Jimmie Davis's attempt at a states'-rights scheme to blunt the federal court's desegregation orders, which failed. In 1962, two public elementary schools in the blue-collar Lower Ninth Ward admitted African American children with U.S. marshals providing security.

Perez had whipped up fervor at rallies, railing against "burrheads." White protesters outside City Hall shouted opposition to desegregated schools. White parents pulled children from schools in neighborhoods where blacks and whites had lived in close proximity. White crowds cursed at the three girls who attended McDonogh No. 19 school in the Lower Ninth Ward. In one of Norman Rockwell's famous paintings, a little black girl named Ruby Bridges walks with big federal marshals to the William Frantz Elementary School door, not far away in the Upper Ninth Ward.

Archbishop Rummel excommunicated Leander Perez from the Catholic Church for his outsized bigotry; the Church later rescinded his expulsion so he could be buried with a Catholic funeral. I was too young to remember those events. But from reading the history, watching news footage of the time, and talking with my father and his friends—particularly Pascal Calogero, his former law partner, who went on to become chief justice of the Louisiana Supreme Court—I came to believe that if we had had enlightened leadership, that embraced the proposition that children of different colors can learn together in the same classrooms, the New Orleans public schools might have been saved, or at least had a chance at success. Instead, we entered the era of white flight to the suburbs. The decades from the 1960s through the '80s changed the demographics of the city and, with it, the schools; the city became poorer and mostly black, and too many people stopped caring about and investing in the public schools.

My mom and dad had nine children in eleven years, starting with Mary (a future U.S. senator) and followed by Mark, Melanie, Michelle, myself, Madeleine (a future judge, now dean of the law school at Loyola New Orleans), Martin, Melinda, and Maurice, Jr. (a future assistant U.S. attorney in New Orleans). We have a run of lawyers—my wife, Cheryl Quirk, is one, as am I. We have been blessed with five children. My parents have thirty-eight grandchildren. My mother can name each one, lickety-split.

The house where I grew up, and where my parents still live, is a raised duplex in the neighborhood called Broadmoor. Broadmoor borders Uptown, which is more middle class and quite prosperous in certain areas, particularly near the Mississippi River and Audubon Park with its beautiful oak trees, and the streets surrounding the campuses of Tulane and Loyola universities, directly across from the park. It took about fifteen minutes by bike for me to reach Audubon Park. Our house had originally been built for two families; as the family grew and my parents knocked down walls to create more bedrooms, they also turned the basement into an apartment for my dad's parents, who joined us in 1966. The family next door had eight kids—their name, confusingly, was Andrieu. Around the corner lived the Osigians; they had fourteen. And around the other corner, the Hennessey family had nine children. That was just two square blocks. In an area of four square blocks, right down the street from where Walter Isaacson grew up, lived the Shirers. They had seven kids. We didn't have to go far to field a team for anything.

Working-class African American families lived the next block over. You have to understand that while New Orleans schools and institutions were segregated, much of the city was geographically a racial patchwork, with black and white families living around the block from each other. Ann Duplessis, who later became a state senator and then came to work with me in City Hall, lived two doors away from us; my dad gave her rides to the Wilson Elementary public school (where most of the black kids went) when he was mayor. Across the street from Ann's home lived the family of Mike Roussell, whose uncle became the first African American provost of Loyola. The Catholic parishes, black and white, were vibrant in those days. I rode my bike to our school, St. Matthias. St. Rita was a five-minute car ride; so was Our Lady of Lourdes on Napoleon Avenue, on the nearer fringes of Uptown, and St. Stephen's, farther down on Napoleon in old Uptown. Holy Name of Jesus, a large church next to Loyola University, stood across St. Charles Avenue from Audubon Park.

That neighborhood in Broadmoor was my window to the world. We played pickup basketball on a goal in our backyard, and touch football on the corner. We played at one another's houses. This is where we were formed—black kids and white kids, in a life that was normal and routine to us. We called one another nicknames—Frog, Carpethead, Big, Turtlehead, Fat, and Rabbit. Today it is hard for me to go anywhere in the city and not run into someone who played ball in our yard or with me on the streets near the house back then. Just kids, just friends, paying no attention to the differences or the color of our skin. Perhaps it was because the black kids I knew were in a similar economic situation. Perhaps it was the seeds my father and mother had planted in all those family conversations.

My mother focused more on us than on things like brand-name clothes or fancy silverware. As I think of it, with nine children she probably had little time for such concerns. We never ate on fine china. We'd drink out of jelly jars that we had emptied when she made peanut butter and jelly sandwiches for us to take to school at St. Matthias, where all nine of us went to lower school. Dad was on the City Council at the time; I remember the blue Pontiac station wagon he drove, with a hole in the floorboard where we used to get our kicks, seeing if we could touch the ground. I look back and realize that even with his law practice and whatever he was pulling in from the part-time city salary, my father had a large family with all the expenses of keeping kids in clothes, food, and school, and that hole in the station wagon floorboard was there because other things came ahead in his list of priorities. Romping around with our friends, devouring the hamburgers and potato salad on picnics at Lake Pontchartrain as the breeze blew in from the lake, were episodes as idyllic as a boy can have.

But during that idyllic time, the world outside my neighborhood was splintering. Today, I look back and doubt the black kids I knew had the same rosy view of the world. As I moved through high school and into college, I pieced together a story of the events that haunted American society before I was old enough to process them—civil rights demonstrations; bitter court battles over segregation; the assassinations of President John F. Kennedy (when I was three), Dr. Martin Luther King, Jr., and Bobby Kennedy, whose funeral on television I vaguely recall my parents watching; the mounting opposition to the Vietnam war; the streets outside the 1968 Democratic Convention, and Chicago police pounding antiwar protesters; the election of Richard Nixon, and then the Watergate scandal. But back then, largely oblivious, I was a happy kid. I had a lot to learn.

My father wasn't the domineering sort who said, "Kids should be quiet." He expected us to engage in conversation. I remember one time at dinner, the phone rang, my sister Melanie answered it, then announced: "There's some idiot on the phone who says he's Governor McKeithen." And my father said, "*Oh, my God.*" It was indeed Governor John McKeithen, a colorful populist, calling from the mansion in Baton Rouge. This was in the early 1970s, when Dad was mayor and they were working together to get the Louisiana Superdome built. "Governor," he said, grabbing the phone, "I'm really sorry, but you know, my kids are pretty unsophisticated."

The governor had a booming laugh. "Moon, we all have kids!"

When I was growing up, my father and I never talked directly about race. I picked up things by osmosis, watching how my parents acted, how they spoke to and treated people. Our house was never closed to anybody. Black children we played with in the neighborhood would come inside with us. One day I was riding in the car with my mother; we were going down Broad Street, near my father's law office, and she stopped the car short. There was a woman lying in the street, and cars were passing her by. She was an African American woman, who was either drunk or incapacitated; she was disheveled and sticking out of her clothes. I remember my mother getting out and helping her get over onto the sidewalk.

The message that the priests at Jesuit High stressed was "men for others." My parents lived that message every day. I remember a day when I was young and got into a fight with an African American friend who lived down the block. His name was Reggie. His parents called my house; my mother came outside. Now, what would you expect your mother to do if you got into a fight with somebody? Take your side! When they told her what happened, my mother said to me: "You were wrong. You need to go tell that little boy you're sorry." I gritted my teeth and I did. I learned at an early age that the entire sense of the household was "Our doors are open. We always help people." And if everybody's welcome, then you're not always the boss. That was the philosophy my mother and father lived by: Be honest, be fair, and everybody's welcome. They never lectured or sat us down and said, "Look, these are the rules." They lived that way; we learned by example.

We didn't get off easy, though. If we got out of line, we caught the belt. My dad would sometimes get upset at us for fighting over petty things, grabbing your sister's or brother's seat at the table, taking something that didn't belong to you, arguing over who sat where watching TV, particularly on Sunday nights when we watched Walt Disney and *Bonanza*—silly stuff that flared into wails and squabbles. He would say, "If you want me to work this out, none of y'all are gonna like it," and in the pluralism of our sprawling household, those words carried weight. It was a really bad situation when Dad said, "Meet me in my room." You really did not want to hear that. Today he claims he doesn't remember ever spanking any of us; but he did, though not badly. My father was anything but harsh. He and my mother have always been there when I needed them, and they both still are today.

In the fullness of time, I have come to realize what extraordinary hearts my parents have, how much they gave us, and others, without making a show of it, how genuinely they respected and enjoyed each other, their children, and other people, whatever they looked like or believed. One time, my oldest sister, Mary, was walking on Broad Street by St. Matthias and saw an African American boy, seemingly cast off. She brought him home. She was fourteen, I was nine. I remember my mother gave him a couch to sleep on and a place at our table until he could be reunited with his family. In a house with nine kids, it was an extraordinary gesture. But that was what we came to expect from our parents, and they expected the same from us.

In 1965, when I enrolled in kindergarten at St. Matthias, the school was all white. On the way to school we walked past Wilson Elementary, the recently desegregated public school, which was nearly all black. New Orleans has historically had a healthy population of African American Catholics. Over the next few years, the first black students arrived at St. Matthias. This was, indirectly, of some consequence to me. On my first day in second grade, a girl I really liked in first grade was gone. When I asked where she was, I learned that her large family had moved to Holy Name of Jesus Parish a couple of miles away, near Audubon Park. Her father didn't want his children going to an integrated school. Holy Name was in an affluent white neighborhood. My heart was broken. I was mad and didn't understand. Our school was great, the kids were great. Her family had lived right around the corner from us. Her father had played on the same high school baseball team as my dad. They had known each other for most of their lives. Her dad stopped talking to my father for some time because my parents kept us at St. Matthias.

As more African American kids came to St. Matthias, more white kids left. The same thing was happening in our neighborhood: white families moving out, black families moving in. "Why aren't we going to Holy Name?" I asked my father. "Because this is where we live," he replied. "This is our neighborhood, and if we leave, the neighborhood's going to be the worse for it. And so would we. We're staying." And so they have, to this day. It is not quite an empty nest; three grandchildren are living with them today.

In 1970, after my father's inauguration as mayor, more people started coming over, to talk, to eat—black people, white people. I met multitudes of people. I was ten years old and I remember leaping into his car on Sunday mornings as he set out to visit churches. One of the most magical moments of my life came at St. Francis de Sales, a Catholic parish on Second Street in Central City, another neighborhood. It was the first time I had heard an African American choir; the sounds were glorious—"Swing Low, Sweet Chariot," "Amazing Grace," "Just a Closer Walk with Thee"—the choral lines swelling up and bouncing off the rafters. I was transported by the way they prayed and praised God in those rolling songs. I remember thinking that their relationship with God was so much more joyous than in the churches where we went to Mass and the people sat in the pews looking bored and couldn't wait to leave after Communion.

I would sometimes hear acquaintances of my parents, or some of our white neighbors, complain about black people as weak, stupid, lazy, criminal, unfaithful, or unpatriotic, often using the N-word, plural. The words rang false to me; they never matched the smart, strong, kind, empathetic, faithful, patriotic, and soulful African Americans I kept meeting. And because certain white friends of the family knew how we felt, they began to look at us in a different way, as if we were weird, or worse. This was when I realized that some grown-ups were flat wrong. I wasn't comfortable challenging them—my parents raised us to be polite, and though my father's politics were on the leading edge of social change, he did not confront or browbeat people in social settings. But if someone gave it to Moon Landrieu, he stood his ground and gave it right back.

The guys I hung with in high school knew where I stood on race; few of them pressed me on it. Our minds were on other things, like the discovery of girls. After I was out of college, though, a friend from Jesuit told me that in high school he was afraid to come to my house because we lived in a black neighborhood. That was strange to me. We lived in a mixed neighborhood, I thought. To some, just like with Homer Plessy, if it was just a little black, a little makes you all black. But I did wonder why white people were afraid of my black friends.

One evening, my father came home from City Hall in a bad mood. Sometimes he came home with a big bag of Lee's Hamburgers (with cooked onions you could smell a block away) and a big smile. But when he got mad, his left eye would twitch, and this night that twitch was in overdrive. It was baseball tryouts. He told us that he had gotten a call from the recreation park supervisor who was in charge of the Carrollton Boosters playground. Each one of us siblings played baseball and volleyball at Carrollton Boosters, a local booster club that sponsored kids' sports. The supervisor had called and told him that some black family was trying to sign up to play ball and the father said he knew us. "Who is the man?" my father asked.

"Some guy named Norman Francis."

My father was livid. He called and eventually fired the supervisor then enrolled his best friend's kids. Michael, David, Timmy, Cathy, Patrick, and Christina Francis were superb athletes who won many an MVP award. But Norman reminded my dad of a sobering truth: "Moon, this cannot just be about my kids."

Under my father's administration, the New Orleans Recreation Department playgrounds welcomed African American kids and dismantled the color barriers for sports teams. The best-selling author Michael Lewis and future NFL star quarterbacks Peyton and Eli Manning all played at Carrollton Boosters.

My wife, Cheryl, grew up in a quiet neighborhood in Metairie, the largely white suburb across the city line in Jefferson Parish. When we met in law school at Loyola in the mideighties, she didn't know Carrollton Boosters existed. After we got married I moved this sweet girl from the suburbs into a mixed New Orleans neighborhood, and I'd brag about Carrollton Boosters. And then literally for the next twenty years, we kept bumping into people who'd tell me, "I remember playing with you at Carrollton Boosters!" Or, "I played with your sister Mary (or your brother Mark) at Carrollton Boosters!" Finally Cheryl said, "Do you know anybody who *didn't* play at Carrollton Boosters?" So when our children were growing up, Cheryl was all in when they started to play at Carrollton Boosters. I coached them all in soccer, baseball, and basketball, getting to relive my childhood. It was a blast.

In my seventh grade and final year at St. Matthias, New
Orleans was hit by a wrenching tragedy. On Sunday, January
7, 1973, my father was having a retreat for his top staff at a
monastery across Lake Pontchartrain outside the town of Cov-
ington. Reports came over the wire that there was a sniper on
top of a building in the Central Business District. My father
rushed back to the house, and by then TV had reports of a
shooter ensconced on top of the Howard Johnson's hotel, just
across Loyola Avenue from City Hall. "I've got to go downtown," said Dad. He had a driver by then. I dove in the back-
seat. I was excited and wanted to be close to the action. My
father didn't know I was there until we got to City Hall; he
took me immediately to the back of the mayor's office and
ordered me not to leave, but I watched it all from his office
window. And though I didn't know it then, it was a foreshad-
owing of some of the domestic terrorism and violence we are
seeing today from Fort Hood to Dallas to Baton Rouge.

The shooter, later identified as Mark Essex, was a twenty-
three-year-old Black Panther sympathizer who had been dismissed from the navy for "character and behavior disorders."
He was on the hotel rooftop, firing at police officers. As the
Times-Picayune would report, Essex had been on the run since
killing a police cadet and wounding a veteran officer a week
earlier in Gert Town, an inner-city neighborhood. In the hotel, in front of room 1829, he shot and killed a Dr. Robert
Steagall and his wife, Betty, who were guests.

He soaked telephone books with lighter fluid and set
them ablaze under the curtains of the Steagalls' room.

On the 11th floor, Essex shot his way into rooms and set more fires. He killed Frank Schneider, the hotel's assistant manager, and shot Walter Collins, the hotel's general manager.

As dusk approached, Essex was trapped in a block house on the hotel roof. The U.S. Marines volunteered a helicopter to get to him. During passes over the roof, officers poured gunfire at the block house while Essex popped out sporadically to fire back.

For hours after they killed him, police searched vainly for a second sniper who they erroneously believed was on the loose. In the days before SWAT squads, the police response was chaotic.

During that tumultuous day, my father had Joe Noto, a big burly police officer with an M16, take me home. When I reached the house, I was struck by the NOPD presence outside. We went downstairs into the basement apartment, where my grandmother was watching TV. She kept asking Mr. Joe how her son was and he kept saying, "He's doing fine, ma'am." The stations were running live news coverage, and just then showed my father running across Loyola Avenue, jumping a barricade, and going into the Howard Johnson's. The lobby had become a command center. In later years he told me it was about the worst day of his two terms as mayor.

Before it was over, Essex killed seven and wounded another eight. Three were police officers. Two other officers had been killed earlier, including one of the great leaders of the police department, Louis Sirgo. To this day, an award in Sirgo's honor is given to the most valuable cadet in the NOPD graduating

class. Guns—and therefore mass killings—were a lot less common in 1973, but the troubling thing is that, just like so often
with mass shootings and politically motivated violence today,
there were warnings. Essex had written a threat letter targeting
police that arrived the day before the rampage.

My parents didn't talk much about the death threats that came
to the house, but every couple of months police would visit
because of threatening calls or a letter. My mother would make
sandwiches that I sometimes delivered to the officers, thanking
them for watching over us. In 1971, after a police shootout with
Black Panthers in the Desire Housing Project, African American protesters had gathered in the street in front of our house
on Thanksgiving Day. We had no police protection then. I
remember sitting outside at the top of the front steps with
several of my siblings, while Dad had talked to some of the
protesters down below. It hadn't exactly been friendly, but he
hadn't called in a security force. I later read in a thesis on my
dad that he'd called the violent wing of the Black Panther Party
"a small group of self-styled revolutionaries." The author,
Frank L. Straughan, Jr., said my dad was in a bind. "They were
not interested in promises of upward mobility in a capitalist
society and rejected compromise, distrusted all authority, and
demanded immediate resolution to longstanding problems.
Worse yet, they were willing to die for their objective."

Two years later, as the Mark Essex tragedy played out, the
police detail was a larger sign to me of how much times had
changed.

Those episodes, etched into my memory, informed for better or for worse some of my views on the police versus community violence of this century. We have to confront the issues

of police behavior, racial profiling, and bias head-on. But despite the injustice, there is no place for violence against law enforcement.

In the spring of 1973 we had to take the entrance test for high school. You were supposed to take it in the school where you wanted to go. I wanted to go to De La Salle, a Catholic high school run by the Christian Brothers, because my older brother, Mark, had gone there. One weekday, my mother attended Mass at St. Matthias. I had this paper to fill out for the high school test. As Mass ended, I told her I needed three dollars. "What do you need it for?" she said.

"This is for my high school thing."

"Let me see that. Mmm. Where you going?"

"I'm gonna go to De La Salle."

"I'll give you three dollars, but put Jesuit down there."

"But I don't want to go to Jesuit."

"Just take the test at Jesuit. And if you get in, you don't have to go."

I took the test at Jesuit, and several weeks later received the letter of admission. "Well," I told my mother, "I'm going to De La Salle."

"No, young man, you are going to Jesuit."

I argued; she would have none of it. Finally, I said, "Mom, *you lied to me!* And we were in church." After a long pause, she said: "Yes. I lied. God's going to forgive me, but you're going to Jesuit." At least she admitted that she lied. She knew the Jesuit teachings would suit my personality and passions.

When I began high school my father's staff was complaining

that he had become too irritable, so to ease the pressure, he decided to take up tennis, which meant getting to the courts at City Park in the early morning before work. I went with him, we played together, and he dropped me at Jesuit before the bell. I got to be a pretty good tennis player, and since it had been suggested to me by certain coaches that my future did not lie in basketball, the tennis team seemed promising. But I had a competing interest by then, and it prevented me from taking up varsity tennis. Since the day I saw *Oliver* at a movie theater, I had been captivated by musicals and had a growing interest in acting. I joined the Jesuit Philelectic Society to perform in stage plays. My parents paid for voice and dance lessons, and by the time I was a senior, I had played Don Quixote in *Man of La Mancha*, Demetrius in *A Midsummer Night's Dream*, Scapino in *Scapino*, and the title role in *Jesus Christ Superstar*. Once you've been Jesus, it's all downhill.

I also performed at the Beverly Dinner Playhouse in Jefferson Parish and got my Actors' Equity card at age sixteen. I was a real professional and landed paid roles in *Fiddler on the Roof* and *Guys and Dolls*, among others. Okay, it might have been local dinner theater, but I had dreams of acting on Broadway, of getting into movies. I occasionally crossed paths with another high schooler, Wynton Marsalis, who was going to Benjamin Franklin, the magnet public high school with a sterling academic record, and taking music lessons in the afternoons at New Orleans Center for Creative Arts, where his dad, the pianist and composer Ellis Marsalis, directed jazz studies. We met when he was in *Shenandoah*, at Le Petit Theatre in the French Quarter, one of the oldest community theaters in the country.

Toward the end of my junior year, I was summoned to the principal's office. Father Harry Tompson and Father Paul Schott were waiting. "Qualifying is about to open for student council president," said Father Tompson. "We think that you have the leadership skills and that you should lead the school. We want you to sign up." I had my hands full doing plays, and not a lot of political aspirations, I told them.

"But you have a responsibility to the school," said Father Tompson.

There was another problem, I explained. One of my closest friends wanted to run for president; his parents had just gotten divorced, and I knew it would help him if he won. "We want you to run," said Father Tompson. "You need to think about it."

"Okay."

Despite the weight of what a Jesuit meant by saying *We*—the priests were custodians of the legacy of a school renowned for its academic and athletic achievements, and its distinguished alumni—I went into a teenager's denial mode, which is to say I ignored it. On the Friday afternoon when qualifying closed, I was rehearsing a play downstairs and the door swung open. Father Tompson came over, stuck his finger in my chest, and said, "It is your responsibility to do the thing that helps the most people in the shortest period of time. You have evaded your responsibility to the students of this school and you should be ashamed of yourself!" He walked out. I was humiliated. I thought, "God, I thought I was doing the right thing, trying to help my friend"—who, by the way, lost the election.

To this day, in every major decision that I have to make, I remember Father Tompson saying *You have a responsibility*—

even if you don't want to do something, even if you didn't create the problem. When you're elected to office, responsibility is an ever-widening territory, often far beyond the political turf you thought was yours.

Father Tompson congratulated me—no hint of a grudge—when I was accepted to Catholic University of America in Washington, D.C., which had a renowned acting program. He left Jesuit to become the director of Manresa House of Retreats outside New Orleans, where I spoke with him many times, and at length, on the retreats I made. We became the closest of friends. In the last years of his life, he became pastor of a church downtown and began a ministry to the poor. Out of that came the Good Shepherd School, a tuition-free school for poor African American students, and, with others, Café Reconcile, which today is the city's best developmental institute for troubled youth, teaching them skills and putting them on a productive path in life. His efforts were focused on the poorest of the poor; and in New Orleans, you can't separate poverty from race.

Here is what I know about race. You can't go over it. You can't go under it. You can't go around it. You have to go through it.

I have been searching for my way through race for all of my conscious life and will keep doing so until God mercifully takes my last breath. The voices across the years, from childhood, through my education, and into public office, speak to me still.

The most important things you learn as the mayor of a city, if you do the job well, are the dynamics of your people, regardless of whether you got their vote. You get to know them by name, by face; you know where they live, where their children go to school. You know their strengths and their weaknesses. You know how the city undulates. You can sense its rhythm and you can feel its backbeat. You know its currents. You know what's spoken and what's unspoken. You feel the city as a human presence in a daily, intimate way.

I believe that the four Confederate monuments in New Orleans that became a dominating presence in my life for well more than two years never reflected what the true society of New Orleans, generations ago, actually felt when they were built. The structures reflected what the people who erected them, mostly ex-Confederate soldiers or sympathizers, believed because they had the power to build them and because they wanted to send a particular political message. They cast a dark and repressive shadow over my city and, in a way, held us back.

It took most of my lifetime to see this. I listened to the words of people who had absorbed a different message from those statues than the one I did over the many years I passed by them with little thought about why they were there. A great part of the territory of governing is listening and learning from your people. And once you do learn the truth about the past, you have a responsibility to act, and so I did.

CHAPTER 2

Learning to See
What's in Front of Me

O n the many mornings I played tennis with my dad in
City Park, we got there by driving down Napoleon
Avenue, and after a few turns, followed South Jefferson Davis Parkway, an avenue with a grassy neutral ground,
toward Canal Street, the thoroughfare that runs from one end
of New Orleans to the other.

In New Orleans, we don't have medians but neutral
grounds. Though I hadn't known it growing up, the words
come from the literal neutral territorial lines of the ethnically
based nineteenth-century municipalities that used to divide
New Orleans, the French Creoles and free people of color on
one side and white Anglo-Americans on the other.

Rarely, if ever, on those drives at sunrise did I pay attention
to the statue of Jefferson Davis, president of the Confederacy,
in a statesmanlike pose atop a granite pedestal facing Canal
Street; I also ignored the name of the street, I guess.

I had, of course, studied the Civil War in school, or so I
thought. The real problem is I wasn't taught much at all. My

middle and high school history classes consisted of lessons about the various battles of the war. We learned that the War Between the States was as much about economics and states' rights as anything, certainly more so than slavery. That fighting for your state was more important back then because the nation was relatively young. There was little to nothing on the morality of slavery, even at Jesuit. Barely a passing mention on Reconstruction. And then not much acknowledgment of Jim Crow before we swiftly moved on to World War I.

I knew that Davis had died in New Orleans in 1889; but on those morning drives in the late 1970s, I had yet to learn that the United Daughters of the Confederacy raised funds to erect the statue, on land donated by the City of New Orleans, in 1911. The Jefferson Davis Memorial Association welcomed any "white person" of good moral character to its ranks, as I read many years later.

I barely even saw the statue; Jefferson Davis was there-but-not-there as we drove by. In countless conversations with white friends and supporters, I've learned that most of them passed the Davis monument in the same mentally distant way. Davis's life was so long ago that it had little bearing on the lives we led. And yet, as I discovered when Confederate monuments became such an explosive issue for me, city officials in 1911 had a strategy for those totemic pieces. They believed in white supremacy. As time passed and racial attitudes changed, their belief still stood there for others to see.

The history we learned was a purposefully false history. Think about this fact: about a quarter of the people in New Orleans in 1911 were African American. They had no voice in the decision; few of them could vote, and even fewer were in any position of political power. As the decades went by, and whites passed the statue with scant interest, Jefferson Davis memorialized a living message for many African Americans.

In 2010, when I was first elected mayor, New Orleans had a 60 percent black citizenry and a rich, flourishing African American culture, vital to our economy. But in the first few years of my term, I honestly didn't think much about the presence of Confederate monuments. The big hurdle was to jump-start the rebuilding process after Hurricane Katrina had left my city on life support.

In 2012, when Trayvon Martin was killed, protests sometimes began and ended at the statue of Jefferson Davis, or in Lee Circle, where Robert E. Lee stands on a huge pedestal at a major traffic juncture. It heated up as the country struggled with police violence from Ferguson to New York to Baltimore. The statues were often "tagged" with spray paint. "Black Lives Matter." "RIP." "BLM." "No justice, no peace." Our departments of property management or sanitation often had to go out to clean the graffiti. The connection did not seem as obvious to me at that point.

Meanwhile, I had begun to talk extensively at home and nationally about the issue of the murders of and by young black men. I was frustrated that there was so much passion and attention being given to police brutality, which was real, and yet very little to something I knew was a sign of the indifference to black lives. The statues seemed like a fringe issue, brought up by a small group of activists from time to time, though they didn't call them symbols of oppression or monuments to white supremacy. To be honest, I didn't fully understand their connection to today's protests. I didn't know my own history.

Jeff Davis—as locals call the parkway—crosses Canal Street and ends a few blocks later at Bayou St. John. That long narrow

body of water, which runs several miles out to the city's northern edge at Lake Pontchartrain, got its name from Jean-Baptiste
Le Moyne, Sieur de Bienville, the French Canadian aristocrat
who founded New Orleans in 1718. Bayou St. John was a vital
artery for the native people before the city came to be. The
point where Jeff Davis ends at the bayou marks the beginning
of Moss Street, which curls along the waterway toward City
Park, which borders on a lovely neighborhood of shotgun
houses and raised cottages with balconies that offer a view of
people canoeing, fishing from the banks of the bayou, flying
kites, or jogging on the grassy strip adjacent to the asphalt. I
adore Moss Street. A few blocks later, you exit Moss with a
left-hand turn and cross the bridge at Esplanade Avenue to
enter City Park.

Outside the park entrance loomed the imposing equestrian
statue of General P. G. T. Beauregard. He led the 1861 attack
by Confederate soldiers on Fort Sumter, which began the Civil
War. He came from a family with deep local roots, and his full
name has a real New Orleans ring: Pierre Gustave Toutant
Beauregard. He died in 1893. The statue was erected in 1915
by an association dedicated to memorializing his military career, with funds again from the city and state.

Ironically, the postwar Beauregard had been an enlightened
voice on race, arguing that "the natural relation between the
white and colored people is that of friendship"—a view that
earned him little white support and cost him some friends. He
became a wealthy railroad executive and lobbyist for the state
lottery.

But the meaning of the Beauregard statue erected by the
monument association had nothing to do with his postwar

advocacy of civil rights. The uniformed general on horseback, the pedestal raised in a small circular garden with flowers, was an absolutely political symbol. Perhaps that is a measure of how a statue succeeds, when it draws your mind from the driver's seat, waiting in traffic, to a signal from the past. In those fleeting moments at the red light where Esplanade Avenue ends at the entrance to City Park, I saw the aesthetic quality of the structure and thought *Confederate leader.* Then as the green light sent us onto the road into the park, Beauregard receded from sight and my thoughts turned to the tennis courts just ahead.

Terence Blanchard also passed the Beauregard statue on his way to school. Two years younger than I, Blanchard, the celebrated jazz trumpeter and composer of Spike Lee film scores, had attended John F. Kennedy High School several miles down, past the northern end of City Park. We wouldn't meet and become friends for many years. Kennedy, as it was called, was a public school with an African American majority student body. In the afternoons, Terence studied jazz under Ellis Marsalis at NOCCA, along with Ellis's son Wynton. He went on to study music at Rutgers, and performed with the Lionel Hampton Orchestra. His breakout came with Art Blakey and the Jazz Messengers. Terence became a young lion of jazz in the 1980s with an international career. Cheryl and I became friends with Terence and his wife, Robin Burgess, who is also his manager, when we were adults.

Terence's encounter as a teenager with that Beauregard statue, on the same route I traveled, left a hard feeling in his gut. To him, it was a monument that denied his humanity; it saluted *the war to keep us slaves.* He told me, "It made me feel less than," and left him bearing down to get through the day.

Whereas I didn't feel much beyond the beauty of a statue memorializing a war that ended a century ago, and a vague pride
that the monument gave New Orleans a European feel.

Terence Blanchard *felt* the weight of history. Long before I
began reading and relearning about New Orleans's booming
antebellum economy as the nation's largest slave market, Terence knew that every day, to get to his high school, named for
the president who championed civil rights in the early 1960s,
he had to pass by a mounted white warrior, a symbol of the
war to preserve slavery. Terence got the message promoted by
the United Daughters of the Confederacy, politicians, and city
officials associated with the Lost Cause all those decades ago.
In their telling, the South had fought a noble war, for honor
and independence, and it would rise from defeat to rule by
white supremacy. Terence got it, he swallowed it, and he
hated it.

That message went right over my head when I was young.
I have often heard it said by elders that you can't know how a
man feels until you walk in his shoes. It has taken me the better part of forty years to find those shoes. This is what I have
come to call transformative awareness. We are all capable of it;
but we come kicking and screaming to a sudden shift in thinking about the past. To get there we have to acknowledge that
we were inattentive, insensitive, myopic, or God forbid, hateful in our earlier view. This is one of the hardest things for
human beings to do, especially when someone calls us on a
belief. It is much easier to make the change when you know
that the person to whom you offer an apology will readily
forgive you, but hard as nails if you think condemnation will
follow.

The shift to a transformative awareness is what John

Newton had in mind when he composed "Amazing Grace" in 1779. Newton was an English slave trader who became so repulsed by the horror and the brutalities he had witnessed that he turned into an antislavery campaigner and wrote the beautiful song as atonement, bequeathing lyrics that are sung today in white and black churches everywhere.

I once was lost, but now I'm found, was blind, but now I see.

People sing this many a Sunday—in black Southern Baptist churches and white Southern Baptist churches, probably at the same moment. Does anyone ever think about the words, or what they mean, or what they are calling us toward? You see, we sing the same song with the same words but don't always derive the same truth. Was I the only one confused by this?

It came to me slowly, in stages, over many years, through encounters that forced me to take a different view of the past. Today, after nearly thirty years of public service, I realize that time and God's grace have helped me appreciate the guides who shared the wisdom of their life episodes to move my thinking along.

Antoine Barriere is pastor of one of the largest African American congregations in New Orleans, Household of Faith Family Worship Church International, which has three locations. Antoine is smart, charismatic, and committed in his ministry's outreach work to those in need. We first met at Jesuit High School; he was a few years behind me, one of the few African American students at the time. As a kid, he was skinny and small. We were friendly, but seniors generally ignored underclassmen. I got to know him well when I became mayor.

A couple of years ago we fell into a conversation about our days at Jesuit. I asked if he had experienced racism. "Not really," he said. He knew some boys who hated blacks; he learned to avoid them. What really pained him was not overt racism. He thought most of the kids were okay, but he said, "In my entire five years at Jesuit, I never once got invited to anyone's house, or to birthday parties, or to just hang out." In other words, he was left alone. Now, I never got left alone. Tons of friends, lots of sleepovers, and I always went to parties. Not Antoine. We were students at the same school. Different color, different outcomes.

When he told me this, I saw pain in the face of a fifty-year-old man, a religious leader and vital community presence; my heart hurt to think of him as a boy back in high school, shunned. He managed to stuff it, just as Terence Blanchard did when passing the Beauregard statue, but it stuck with him. Walk in their shoes, and you begin to feel the far-reaching implications of all the big and little ways that some of us had it better than others, and how that played out. Race is a powerful force in how our minds respond to the past, and a key to America's splintered politics today.

Like it or not, we all carry the past of our country. The unresolved conflicts of race and class lay coiled, ready to erupt, unless we set our minds to an honest reckoning with that past and a search for solutions grounded in genuine truth and justice. Unlike the cursing anonymous voice on a telephone, or the menacing face, or the billy club that split John Lewis's head in Selma, Alabama, at the Edmund Pettus Bridge in 1965, implicit bias is hard to see; implicit bias is a silent snake that slinks around in ways we don't notice.

Questions gather at the threshold of transformative awareness. Whom do we sit with at lunch? Who are the kids we invite to our children's parties? Or look at for honors programs at school? Who do we think of as smart, with good moral fiber, God-loving and patriotic? To whom do we give the benefit of the doubt, and why? Who are the people we condemn most quickly? As questions multiply about the consequences of race, it forces you to look in the mirror and see yourself as you really are, not who you've been told you are, not who society has made you to be, and not the image you want others to perceive. That's when you start noticing things about yourself you never thought about before. The sight is not always pretty.

The big question for me as high school drew to a close was where to apply for college. I really had no idea. My older siblings had gone to in-state universities. With four siblings behind me, I knew my parents would be pressed to provide tuitions and college living expenses. The mayor's salary in 1978 was $25,000, which converts to a value of about $97,000 today. (The salary today is $163,000.) As his term was ending, though, Dad had been offered a job with a downtown real estate developer and a corporate salary that would make a huge difference for the family—and college for me.

My decision came in the winter of 1978 through a comic epiphany during Mardi Gras season. As a high school senior, I accompanied my parents to the ball for Bacchus, a Mardi Gras parade "krewe," in local parlance, which had begun just nine years before. Founded by, among others, Owen Brennan of the Brennan restaurant family, Bacchus recruited businessmen, many of whom lacked the social ties for admission to the patrician men's clubs that sponsored the parades and balls. For as much as everything is about race, it can also be about class. For the old-line krewes, your lineage mattered. Upstart Bacchus invited the comedian Danny Kaye to ride as its first king, in-augurating a practice of "celebrity kings" that caught on with several other parades. Raymond Burr, Bob Hope, Jackie Glea-son, Glen Campbell, and Henry Winkler soon followed Danny Kaye in that monarchy. In 1978, the Bacchus king was Ed McMahon, the rollicking sidekick to Johnny Carson on *The Tonight Show*. At the ball that followed the parade, I ended up sitting at the same table with Ed McMahon. To the best of my recollection, McMahon said, "So, what's your game plan, fel-low?" I said I was graduating in the spring from Jesuit and hoped to study acting.

"Acting!" said the television comedian. "You should go to Catholic University in Washington, D.C. Great acting pro-gram! That's where I went!" He went on about his college days, riffing about the drama program and dropping names of other alums like Susan Sarandon and Jon Voight, reminding me with a wink that he had risen from CU to the throne of Bacchus, and then with a hint of mischief said, "The archbishop is on the board."

Philip M. Hannan, archbishop of New Orleans, had come to town from Washington, D.C., in the midsixties. As a mili-tary chaplain in World War II he had parachuted into Ger-many. He was a friend of the Kennedy family and spoke at President Kennedy's funeral Mass. A liberal leader on issues of race and social justice, he was a New Dealer of sorts, building a network of homes for the elderly, expanding the work of Associated Catholic Charities. A popular figure in New Or-leans, Hannan had a low-key personality and Irish amiability in one-on-one conversations, and was a good friend of my parents'.

Archbishop Hannan, it turned out, was not only on the

Catholic University of America board, but had the authority to award a scholarship each year to any student of his choice. With his support, I went off to Washington, D.C., in the fall of 1978 as a freshman at Catholic U. By then, I had a premonition that I would be a lawyer; but my interest in theater still ran deep, and Father Gilbert Hartke's program was remarkable, to say the least. Catholic U. operated under a pontifical mandate from the Vatican. It attracted students from more blue-collar and middle-class families than Georgetown University across town, which was run by Jesuits and had many students from comparatively affluent families.

CUA worked well for me. I liked the fact that classes were comparatively small. Norman Ornstein was my adviser in political science, and remains a friend. He's now a resident scholar at the American Enterprise Institute, and go-to interviewee of the media on issues relating to Congress and national politics. The tennis coach at Catholic U was Marty Dowd. (His sister, Maureen Dowd, was a 1973 CUA graduate just breaking in as a reporter with the *Washington Star*, starting on the road that led to her becoming a *New York Times* columnist.) I approached Marty Dowd on the tennis court and told him I wanted to join the team.

"Did you play in high school?" he asked.

"I've been playing for years but I wasn't on a team," I shot back.

"I have been recruiting for months and didn't see you. You really have to leave."

"Look, who's your best player?"

He motioned to a guy at the far end of the court.

"If I beat him, can I be on the team?"

"Go try," he challenged.

I took the set and made the team, though I was the least talented player. Catholic U was small enough to allow someone like me to pursue overlapping interests without the pressure that exists in a major university, where being an athlete was like a full-time job when you weren't in class or studying. I took voice lessons, became involved in student politics, and got rare insights on Washington through Father Hartke. He was close friends with Helen Hayes, and had been a mentor to John Slattery, who went on to become a star in *Mad Men*, *Will and Grace*, *Sex and the City*, and many other shows.

I was carrying a full academic load, but when Father Hartke asked me to be his driver, I readily agreed. We would head downtown in a blue station wagon to Duke Zeibert's restaurant, a hub for power lunches. Father Hartke would make the rounds, glad-handing with guests to raise funds for expenses to send his kids on USO tours, performing for the American military in foreign countries. Bob Hope was a mainstay of USO shows and was close to Father Hartke. In the summer before my junior year I tried out for the USO and was accepted. I was also chosen to join a group of CUA theater students in partnership with a drama program in Poznan, Poland. I taught the history of American musical theater.

Being a part of entertaining the troops and traveling in Europe was a glorious experience, exposing me for the first time to the architecture, museums, and living legacy of Western civilization. I also saw the boot heel of Communism in Poznan. Pope John Paul II, the first Polish pope, was a national hero in the country that the Nazis invaded, and that after the war began a dark night of the soul under Soviet Marxist rule. The communist economy hindered market growth; a secret police had tentacles reaching deep, arresting people who dared to question the system. The regime forced newspapers to toe the party line, and otherwise muzzled free speech. I befriended Polish students, who conveyed their frustration in sometimes cautious ways. I had never felt so strangely privileged.

The streets were tense. Soldiers with automatic weapons were on patrol. Lech Wałęsa, the founder of Solidarity, the first independent trade union behind the Iron Curtain, was driving a movement for greater freedom, in frequent trouble with authorities, and an inspiration to the Polish people for it. I met students who thirsted for freedom. These kids were smarter than we were, they spoke languages we didn't know, they sang along to American rock songs in perfect English at Polish nightclubs. They wanted American jeans. It was startling and a bit humbling to realize how much we took for granted, in the abundance of American life and in our basic freedoms, which these kids craved.

I was accustomed to a robust media, raucous political campaigns, and liberty in artistic expression in drama, film, and literature, all elemental to American identity. I saw how much Polish students my age hungered for these freedoms and how much the repression stunted the country's growth.

That summer in Poland, an inner voice kept telling me, *You have to go to Auschwitz,* where the Nazi death camp had been preserved. I am not sure how that voice originated. New Orleans was home, a place of love for me, yet I had also seen there hatred in a grinding, personal way, including in my father's struggles to bring African Americans into New Orleans politics and the ugly blowback our family endured.

I am not sure anyone is ever prepared to visit a museum created by genocide, whether it's in Germany, Rwanda, or Cambodia. These places exist because of the evil incarnate in our lives, and because a basic morality insists that we remember the victims and that we resolve to work against the poisonous hatred that uses mass murder as a weapon of politics. I was barely twenty when I visited Auschwitz. I clearly remember the suitcases stacked high bearing the names of people gassed to death, men and women and children who never knew that their meager belongings would one day signify their lives. The mounds of hair, hairbrushes, false teeth, prosthetics, the stacks of eyeglasses, they carried a moral weight heavier than anything I had ever felt. To read about the Holocaust from afar is to get a grasp on history and that unspeakable horror. It also allows denial to creep in—*That was then, this is now. It is not us. This can never happen in the United States.* But when you stand in the very place where so many human beings were murdered in one of the world's worst atrocities, you wonder how a group of people could become so cruel. And then to see the ovens. My God—the ovens.

We were taught, growing up, that man was basically good, but that evil is a force that must be resisted. Although you learn about the Holocaust in school, how is a kid supposed to come to grips with the notion that human beings could be so evil as to trap and incinerate millions of their fellow human beings? This is not a rhetorical question; the answer is far from simple. The Nazi ideology dehumanized Jews to such a point that the industry of mass murder relied on numbed obedience. Did Hitler's volcanic hatred seep like acid into the soul of the Nazis who ran Auschwitz and other death camps? How did mass brainwashing happen? My head felt like it was exploding. The message of the museum, "Never again," kept reverberating in my mind. *We can't let this happen again.*

And then the realization came that we had done something

like this in America with slavery. The systemic evil of Nazism was the closest thing to the Southern society that relied on slave labor. I was torn by the connection between these two realities of history, different in time and place, but with a common root, a warped sense that some people are superior to others, a supremacy trapped in its own frozen heart.

The Civil War that I rarely thought about had ended more than a century ago, yet in 1979, I knew the seeds of hatred were still fertile back home, the anger and prejudice still alive. I remember my heart growing a bit colder that day, my vision clearer, the proof of man's capacity to do horrible, wicked things in what my own eyes had seen. Hate unchecked knows no bounds, and when it rises up it must be confronted and rejected or it will spread like an endless cancer. I had not yet thought about why there were no markers of the atrocities committed on our land, in our city. Why no slave ship markers? Why no plantation histories told through the eyes of the enslaved Africans who worked them? That would come to me later.

Auschwitz laid a foundation, a building block, in my mind, not only for how evil humans can be to one another, but also for how we can reckon with and learn from our past so as to not repeat the same mistakes in the future. That day I prayed that if I was ever tested by the power of evil, I would have the courage to stand for what was right.

In 1979 President Jimmy Carter offered my father the position of secretary of Housing and Urban Development in his cabinet, and the year and a half Dad spent in Washington overlapped with the middle of my undergraduate years at Catholic

University. I was glad to be away from home, experiencing life in a new place. Washington had several major theaters; I was making strides as a double major, in political science and theater. Still, I missed my family, so it was nice to spend time with my father. One night he confided that although running HUD was demanding, "it's a lot easier than being mayor." The federal bureaucracy moved at a much slower pace. After meetings with mayors and city or county officials to work out agreements for federal assistance in major building projects, the applications added another layer of time for internal review on a given contract. Nothing happened fast, whereas governing a city meant responding to *people* daily on issues that affected their lives.

My mother stayed in New Orleans, with a house full of my younger siblings to manage. My dad flew home most weekends; he rented a condo on Seventh Street, in Southwest D.C., not far from his office. I spent occasional evenings with my father, and from time to time visited him at the HUD office. But although I followed the 1980 presidential campaign through the *Washington Post*, I avoided Capitol Hill and had a more abstract interest in politics that was satisfied by certain courses I took.

Near the end of my undergraduate years, I spent an Easter break on campus, working on my thesis on affirmative action. (I had done another paper for my drama course on Arthur Miller, focusing on *Death of a Salesman*, *The Crucible*, and *All My Sons*—plays that were prescient on issues of culture and the white working class that were relevant to today's politics.) On a break from the writing I played a pickup game of basketball in the gym, two-on-two, with three guys I didn't know. My teammate was white, the other pair African Americans. The game got a little rough, a couple of elbows collided, and I went down on the hardwood floor. A black guy stood over me and called me "a blond-haired blue-eyed devil." I looked up at his face and had a mental flashback ten years earlier to that woman calling my father a "nigger lover" on the steps of the Jesuit gym. It hit me that this courtside slur was the first time anyone had challenged me solely on the basis of my race.

Picking myself up, I said, "What are you talking about? You don't even know me. It's just a basketball game." We went ahead and finished, with no more words exchanged, but the moment shadowed me for days. I'd spent my first twenty years with white buddies kidding me that I was more black than white, and African American friends embracing me as a straight shooter without racial prejudice. Now in a college pickup game of basketball, race becomes a player? I had played hundreds of basketball games in my backyard with black boys and no one ever spit hate-eyes like that guy did at me. And then it hit me. I learned that day that black people can be blinded by race, too.

As college graduation neared, my father offered to cover the law school tuition at Loyola if I returned to New Orleans. I still wanted to make a go of it as an actor. "I don't want to say you can't succeed," he said gently. "But it's a hard road. With a law degree, you can get a job and raise a family."

I promised to think about it. I made a trip to New York. I had a few friends and some contacts through the network of Catholic alumni working in theater. I showed up at an audition with two hundred guys who looked taller and more handsome than I. It seemed unlikely that a director would somehow pick me. As the realization sank in, I thought about the hard life of young actors and actresses, waiting tables, hustling from one audition to another, searching for a break—not just the big break, but *any* break leading to steady work. My confidence sank as I thought about what it would take to launch a career in theater—a lot of hit-and-miss work. I knew that at some point I'd want to marry and have kids. New York is one of the most exciting places in the world, a city I have loved since the first of many visits in my college years. But for me at twenty-one, pondering the crossroads, the idea of a struggling artist's life fast lost its appeal.

On the first day of classes at the Loyola law school in fall of 1982 I met a girl named Cheryl Quirk, who had a killer smile but politely responded to my interest by letting me know she was wholly unavailable.

I was living at home again, raking leaves as part of the deal, wishing I had enough to take an apartment; but with my dad paying the tuition, and no charge for my mother's meals, the deal was too good. I was spending lots of time in a study group and at the library and, of course, back at the Beverly Dinner Playhouse, where I'd gotten my first professional gig.

One morning as I was about to push off to school, my father said that Jimmy Carter was coming to town to hold a fundraiser for his presidential library in Atlanta. Just before the appointed day, the major donor who was hosting the event had a heart attack. My dad had been working hard to line up guests. Mr. Carter said, "Moon, can you do it at your house?" Ever the loyalist, my father said of course. This threw the home into chaos. My mother, who still had no interest in fine china or wine stems, was suddenly going to host a former president at our house on South Prieur Street with the endless bedrooms and still some bunk beds. My oldest sister, Mary, had been elected to the legislature and helped with the emergency organizational details. In the middle of the preparations—with four of the nine children still at home, we had to ensure that everyone was on time and no one brought friends home for supper—the Secret Service arrived to sweep the house. I went with my father to the airport and was delighted to see that effusive Jimmy Carter smile. The event went off well, and at the end of the evening Mr. Carter accepted my parents' invitation to spend the night. I was a little amazed that he didn't want to stay at the Royal Orleans or a major downtown hotel. Surrounded by a small army of Landrieus, he sat on the couch, slipped off his shoes, and talked away like a visiting uncle.

My parents had moved their bedroom to the basement, next to the room where my late grandparents had lived. When he was ready to turn in, I escorted him downstairs, and asked something that had been eating at me all night: "Sir, of all the people you worked with, who was the greatest?"

"Anwar Sadat," he replied. "The world will never fill his shoes."

Mr. Carter was a runner. The next morning he got up early to jog and invited me to join him. The limousine headed quietly to Audubon Park where *Times-Picayune* editor Charles Ferguson, a friend of Dad's, met us with a photographer and reporter. I did a lap of the park, jogging with Jimmy Carter. Then we drove back to the house; he took a shower, thanked us all, and left. The Secret Service picked up their equipment, and within twenty-four hours it seemed almost as if nothing had happened. I went off to law school in a daze.

During my final year of legal studies I persuaded Cheryl Quirk to take me seriously, and we were soon wonderfully in love. After graduation we both got coveted law clerk jobs, she for the state's Fourth Circuit Court of Appeal, and I for Louisiana Supreme Court justice Pascal Calogero, my dad's old law partner. In short order, Cheryl and I were married and I began a law practice. I hadn't really thought much about getting into politics, but an opportunity came up that I found too tempting to pass up. Mary had graduated from Louisiana State University in 1977, became a real estate agent in 1979, and ran for the seat in the state legislature that included the Broadmoor neighborhood where we had grown up. It was the same seat my dad had held in the dark days of Jimmie Davis and Leander Perez. Mary went door-to-door throughout the area and won the election at age twenty-three. Eight years later, in 1987, she advised me that she was going to give up the seat to run for state treasurer. Besides offering my support to her for the new position, I decided to run for the seat she was vacating.

When you grow up in a political family, particularly one as large as ours, neighborhood campaigning becomes a regular social ritual. Knocking on the doors of people you know, asking for support, is a way of reminding them that yes, you remember them, as they say, *I saw you back when your daddy was running and you were way little!* Handing out flyers, talking with people on sidewalks and shopping malls is a great learning experience. You learn that your older sister did a good job of contacting people and responding to their needs. Some faces light up, people who are delighted to talk. You also spot people half a block ahead who put their heads down, signaling that they want no eye contact and, God knows, they certainly don't want to talk. Is it because I'm a Landrieu, or because they just don't like politics?

My dad's popularity and my parents' long presence in the district, which included more affluent Uptown neighborhoods across South Claiborne Avenue from our house, was a tremendous advantage to Mary in her first race, and to me when I began mine. But it's daunting to run to fill your sister's legislative seat. If you lose, shame on you, boy.

Cheryl had not grown up this way. Her upbringing in Metairie was upper middle class, much more conventional and far less political. Her parents were conservative, but welcomed me as lovingly as a son-in-law could want. Cheryl jumped into the campaign with zeal; she was pregnant with our first daughter, Grace (just as my mother, Verna, had been carrying me when Dad won the district in 1960). Cheryl walked with me several times, standing beside me as I rang bells, asking people for their support, giving them campaign literature, hoping they embraced the message.

The district was 55 percent white and 45 percent African American, yet my only major opponent was white as well. The white sections of the district were more affluent. We were generally well received; however, after several weeks, Cheryl said, "The poorer people are more open and invite you into the house. They even offer us food."

Some of the wealthier homes had private guards, but they rarely kept us out; but boy, watch out if you interrupt a cocktail hour! I would regularly call my dad with an update on how things were going. He would wax nostalgic about his early years of campaigning, and how he always stopped in neighborhood bars to shake hands and meet voters. Several times I wanted to say, "But, Daddy, that was *twenty-eight* years ago." Little did I know.

There was of course no Internet in 1979, or social media, but TV and radio spots were overtaking the folkways of retail campaigning, sad to say. My father kept suggesting that I make sure to go into neighborhood bars. I ignored him. He kept bearing down on me—*Go into those bars!* So finally I did, a corner barroom that had been a watering hole for the same guys for the last fifty years. Lots of cigarette smoke. Bottles of beer lined up on the bar. You get the picture. I sidled up to one old-timer and said, "Hi, my name is Mitch Landrieu. I'm running for state representative and I sure would like your vote!" The guy glared at me. "I hate your father. He ruined the city when he gave it over to the blacks. I would *never* vote for you."

I learned a valuable lesson that day: Never campaign in a barroom full of drunk guys who hate Landrieus. That night I talked to my dad, told him I had hit a few bars, and that we were doing great. I never campaigned in a barroom again. I won that election, winning the primary by 51 votes, and my political career began.

CHAPTER 3

David Duke and Donald Trump, a Nightmare Loop

The Louisiana State Legislature occupies the main floor of the Louisiana State Capitol Building, a thirty-four-story office tower, distinguished by Art Deco design, built in the early 1930s under Governor Huey P. Long. The building houses various state offices and looms like a monolith over scenic lakes, the Governor's Mansion, and downtown Baton Rouge, all along the Mississippi River. The Capitol is awe-inspiring for its size and beauty, not to mention the Huey Long statue, looking defiant, out on the lawn lined by oak trees. In that majestic building, I remembered how my father had been threatened in 1960 for taking a stand against Jim Crow laws, and upon taking my oath of office in 1988, I took comfort in how far race relations had advanced since that dark time.

I found a camaraderie with other legislators rallying around a new reform governor, Democrat Charles "Buddy" Roemer. We entered the legislature with one of the best groups elected in Louisiana—people like Randy Roach of Lake Charles; Sean

Reilly, Melvin "Kip" Holden, and Raymond Jetson of Baton Rouge; Charles Riddle of Marksville; all representatives dedicated to politics that make a difference in people's lives. President Ronald Reagan's popularity had caused a number of Democratic officials to switch parties and become Republicans, but Louisiana still had a strong statewide Democratic majority. The guys in my group felt we were part of a New South dawning. Next door in Mississippi, Governor Ray Mabus, a Harvard Law School alumnus and a Democrat, was trying to steer a reform agenda of his own. And Governor Bill Clinton in Arkansas, a graduate of Georgetown and Yale Law School, shared the vision of a South moving past its old, bitter divisions of race and class.

The state was nearly bankrupt when Roemer took office; stabilizing the tax structure was a pivotal early issue. Our team focused on a socially progressive but fiscally responsible agenda. And unlike the bitter partisan divide today, we put together a coalition of Democrats and Republicans to pass a statewide sales tax to balance the budget. Louisiana had a system of public hospitals linked to Charity Hospitals in New Orleans and Baton Rouge, which we also reorganized under the LSU School of Medicine system to streamline efficiency in services and finances.

Louisiana has abundant natural resources, beautiful land, and a thriving culture of wonderful people, bighearted and big souled. Nevertheless, the state was near the top of all the "bad" lists—the national rankings of shortest life expectancy, low-birth-weight babies, infant mortality, poverty, obesity, illiteracy, and incarceration—and near the bottom on the "good" lists—college graduates and new jobs created. Politically, we had been so hobbled by corruption as to undercut the purpose of government—to deliver services to help people improve their lives, educate their children, make a good living, and find prosperity in their jobs and businesses.

On the eighty-mile drive from New Orleans to Baton Rouge, as Lake Pontchartrain receded and Interstate 10 passed lush, semitropical foliage, I kept thinking about the divide between so much poverty, in pockets many people never saw, and the beauty of the bayous, the oak-lined parks, the lakes and Gulf channels where people fished, and the festivals where people danced and served grand food, embracing *laissez les bon temps rouler*—let the good times roll. Before they rose to the middle class, people of Cajun and Creole communities found a way to love life and celebrate death, to dance in the face of the devil and let the joy of living permeate their lives.

And yet as a political matter, race and poverty can hardly be separated. As we often see today, the common strategy during the decades of segregation was to scare poor whites into thinking that blacks and other minorities were their enemies, when in fact they all faced the same economic hurdle. When you enact a policy, pass a law, impose a tax, or grant a tax break, the repercussions that reach down the socioeconomic scale may be subtle at first, but the impact can be real. The state recovery sales tax we eventually passed under Roemer staved off massive cuts to education and health care, which would have disproportionately affected lower-income families, since these are services poor people—black and white—depend on.

On that day at Auschwitz in the summer of 1980, I committed to fight against bigotry and hatred if I ever confronted it. I could never have known how quickly it would stare me directly in the face. In the summer and fall of 1988, as Vice President George H. W. Bush ran for president against Massachusetts governor Michael Dukakis, an obscure candidate named David Duke competed first for the Democratic slot, and then for the Populist Party, a white nationalist fringe group. Born in Oklahoma, a Ku Klux Klan Grand Wizard in the 1970s, Duke wore a coat and tie like any other candidate, pitching an appeal to disaffected whites on issues such as affirmative action, welfare reform, and set-aside guarantees for minority contractors on public building projects at a certain level. Duke's "issues" were a coded way of masking his longtime racial bigotry. Like most people, I gave no thought to Duke as a presidential candidate. Elections large and small attract all kinds of people willing to pay the filing fees and run for office, with not a chance to win, yet hoping for media attention to their personalities or causes. When his name occasionally popped up, I dismissed him as a hate-mongering quack. During the Louisiana Democratic presidential primary, he aired a thirty-minute paid political ad in which he spoke like a serious candidate with carefully worded messages on his core themes, particularly welfare. He got 23,390 votes, or 3.8 percent of the total votes cast, in that state primary. On the national Election Day, he won 48,267 votes, or .05 percent, on the Populist ticket. Where does a presidential candidate go after such a poor showing?

The answer came a few months later, in early 1989, when a State House seat became vacant in Metairie, the nearest suburb to New Orleans in neighboring Jefferson Parish. David Duke jumped into the race even though, as we later learned, he didn't even live in the district.

Metairie was like many white-flight suburban areas outside

cities. Cheryl grew up on one of its quiet streets and loved it. Metairie also had wealthy enclaves with expensive homes, and a strip of wonderful small restaurants in Bucktown, an area along Lake Pontchartrain that had once been a fishing village. Demographically, the district was also full of people who left the city to avoid integrated public schools, have safer streets, and try to retain a semblance of the close neighborhoods they knew growing up. Some were afraid, and moved for reasons of race; others, for economic reasons and greater opportunity. It was all part of a massive national shift in population to the expanding suburbs, where the Nixon and Reagan administrations allocated greater federal resources, thus reshaping politics over the next fifty years. The trend is reversing today, as more people are moving into cities. The political transformations will be equally profound. The great policy test at hand is to strike a balance in federal support of cities and rural towns, and to stabilize the federal budget in order to do so.

There was little media interest in an off-year suburban legislative race, but Duke was impressing people at candidates' forums, and as the primary unfolded, stories about his bizarre back pages made some reporters begin to take interest.

In 1970, as an LSU undergraduate in Baton Rouge, Duke had paraded in a Nazi uniform at the university's "Free Speech Alley," where speakers on any topic have a forum. He was protesting an appearance by William Kunstler, the radical lawyer who was defending demonstrators who had been arrested at the Democratic Convention in Chicago. Sporting a swastika on his sleeve, Duke carried a sign that read GAS THE CHICAGO 7. In most states a photograph like that dredged up from a candidate's past would be a political obituary. But Louisiana has its own ideas about what works in politics (see under: Huey

Long and Edwin Edwards). He was tapping a vein of anger and fear, injecting race into the campaign, which the other candidates didn't want to exploit, and in a sinister way his notoriety benefited him. When called to account for the 1970 protest—some people actually called him "The Nazi of LSU"—he brushed off as "youthful mistakes" the jaded theatrics of an anti-Semite. He kept steering his message back to welfare abuse, affirmative action, and minority set-asides, attacking people of color but in smoother language than in his Ku Klux Klan days. The hate hadn't changed; the message was just more softly packaged, trading on stock GOP issues and its core Southern Strategy. His job was to persuade people that he wasn't who he was.

In 1980, Ronald Reagan had declared in a speech in Philadelphia, Mississippi—where the Ku Klux Klan had murdered three civil rights workers in 1964—"The South will rise again!" As president, he promoted tax breaks for segregated Southern academies and tried to substitute pickle relish for vegetables in school lunches. Those measures failed, but the attempt itself sent a signal to a white Southern base. Richard Nixon had pioneered the Southern Strategy, milking the region's oldest fear, courting whites who resented the federal courts for altering their way of life. The idea that the South bore any responsibility for the long, cruel domination of blacks was papered over, casting African Americans as both aggressors and victims of their own vices. In a very real sense, the Republican Party's hard right tilt played into Duke's hands.

Duke worked hard to present himself as an unflappable candidate, speaking in reasoned cadences, telling people who asked about his years in the KKK that he had "evolved" in his views, using TV news to project an image of cool and calm.

The tacit rule of news coverage for local elections of this kind was to be balanced in allotting time and focus on the major candidates, without going overboard in deep reporting on anyone. Few heard, then, about Duke's background.

A weird script was emerging, one I had not seen before—a politician's ability to promote himself as new and different, broken loose from a vicious past, as if the past had almost never happened. He tempered questions about his Klan activity by denying facts or shading reality. When I look back today, David Duke's demagoguery stands like a dress rehearsal for the rise of Donald Trump. While he may not have worn a hood or swastika, Trump's rhetoric and actions during his 2016 presidential campaign were shockingly similar to the tactics deployed by Duke in 1989. Because of their outlier status, both candidates got loads of free media coverage that allowed them to define themselves. With Steve Bannon's help, Trump cultivated a base of white nationalists, many of whom are Nazis, in or out of the closet, as we saw in the June 2017 Charlottesville, Virginia, riot.

As journalists began digging up Duke's past, we learned of a numbing record of associations with Nazis, home-grown fascists, anti-Semites, hate groups, and Klan members. But the information emerged in fits and starts, and during those winter weeks in Metairie in 1989, the overshadowing factor was Duke's telegenic skill, the power of the demagogue to push a message—blame the other; the problem is blacks. Duke also had an extraordinary hatred for Jews, which he did his best to mask.

Like the economic angst felt by people today that propelled Donald Trump, Louisiana had a 10 percent unemployment rate, the nation's highest at the time, when Duke emerged as a political lightning rod. But for all of the raw feelings among white people on the economic edge amid the state recession, the Metairie district was largely affluent, a mix of traditional Republicans and Reagan Democrats, people who kept their old party affiliation while supporting a popular GOP president. What did they see in Duke?

"We need him now," a New Orleans Country Club member, who naturally requested anonymity, told *Times-Picayune* columnist Iris Kelso. "We have to send a message to the blacks." A message—the same stale, old logic of the Lost Cause supporters who put up the Jefferson Davis statue in 1911 as a symbol of white control, white power. What did that message mean now? That crime, teenage pregnancies, and violence bred of poverty would not be tolerated? That welfare victimized white people—when many (if not many more) whites relied on the same assistance?

The parallels between David Duke and President Trump, as demagogues, are breathtaking. Duke shadowboxed with his past to suggest he wasn't a hardened bigot; many white voters in the district liked him for "standing up" to blacks—an issue that had little bearing on the needs of that suburban district. Trump has found a way to depict Mexicans and immigrants as rapists and criminals; urban cities as dark, crime-ridden places; black athletes as unpatriotic; refugees as welfare and government-assistance mongers. Trump's Make America Great Again slogan is the dog whistle of all times. The meaning is deeply hidden in the words to the unassuming eye and ear but comes on like a freight train to those who are attuned to its meaning. It seems so benign, but the word *again* gave the line its punch. *Again* fills African Americans with dread. Exactly when were we great before? What are we going back to? And by the way, your *great* wasn't so great for me.

To people in the falling middle class, whether in Appalachia, the Deep South, the Rust Belt, or other areas where factory jobs had dried up, Make America Great Again sent a message: restore the America whose booming postwar economy saw factory workers buy houses and secure a middle-class life. But the massive shift from an industrial economy to the digital revolution, with factories closing and companies sending jobs overseas—can't be reversed by the mere waving of a presidential wand. Retraining people for a new economy takes government investment, just as the GI Bill of Rights gave soldiers returning from World War II college tuition to get an education that positioned them for good employment. The social Darwinists running today's Republican Party don't believe in government programs like that. Trump's macho theatrics had a galvanizing appeal, but when you get down to meat on the table, what has Trump—or this Republican-majority Congress—done to uplift those working-class Americans?

The other ring in Trump's "make us great" mantra—his attack on Muslims—played that same screechy fiddle, fanning fear—blame the other. "Make America Great Again" carries a coded mantra: make America white again. David Duke crowed to that fiddle more than any politician I ever encountered until I watched the rise of Trump. He plays on fear of the other, on us versus them, which frankly I thought was done after we sent David Duke packing.

Duke made his living off a bizarre organization called the National Association for the Advancement of White People (you'll get the reference). He ran the NAAWP with mass-mail marketing and subscriptions to a periodic newspaper that included a long list of mail-order books, some of which debunked the Holocaust as a myth. It didn't take much time perusing NAAWP material for me to realize that Duke, even if he had cut his ties to the Klan, was a white supremacist, a fascist, and probably a Nazi, though proof of that was border-line at the time. Much later, a *Times-Picayune* reporter de-scribed him as "a self employed career fundraiser." The struggle it took, by many people over several years in Louisi-ana, to push Duke back into his cave of lies and warped beliefs, is a story worth recalling today.

Many people in New Orleans resentfully remember my father's tenure as mayor in the seventies as the time when African Americans got jobs in the city government and a greater profile in politics. That is certainly true; but it was also a time of comparative affluence across racial lines—the whole city was booming. Downtown, Poydras Street saw construc-tion of hotels and office buildings. Various capital projects else-where in town included restoration of the French Market, while new houses went up in the suburbs of New Orleans East, all amid a general increase in African American employment. Lyndon Johnson's Great Society initiative in the 1960s still carried over in revenue-sharing funds under the Nixon admin-istration. Reagan famously said that he ended the war on pov-erty because "poverty won." A great sound bite, but how true? Consider the analysis of the historian Kent Germany, in his deeply researched study *New Orleans After the Promises: Poverty, Citizenship, and the Search for the Great Society*:

> The question of who won the War on Poverty has dominated the examination of the Great Society's legacies. The one undeniable fact is that the official

poverty rate did decline in the United States. It fell from 19 percent in 1964 to a low of 11.4 percent in 1978, rising to 13.1 by 1989. The rate was at 11.3 in the year 2000. In Louisiana, the rate fell from 26.3 percent in 1969 to 18.6 percent in 1979 before rising to 23.6 percent in 1989. By 2000, it was 19.6 percent. In New Orleans, the city's overall poverty rate was actually higher in 2000 (at 28 percent) than in 1960 (at 25 percent), attributable partly to demographic shifts. The local black poverty rate, however, fell dramatically from 50 percent in 1960 to near 30 percent in 2000. . . .

Although the Great Society did not dramatically alter the foundations of poverty, it was a much better attempt to improve living conditions and public participation for marginalized people than had ever been attempted before, and, arguably, it contributed to the economic growth that many politicians and academics claim was responsible for the decline in poverty.

The Great Society lifted many people out of poverty, and I am one mayor who remembers. How many more people on the margins might have reached a better place had the programs continued, we don't know. I saw the changes in New Orleans over the years before Duke began peddling his false version of the past. In the 1980s, Reagan started slashing programs and forced the mayor after my dad, Ernest "Dutch" Morial, to cut city jobs; that loss of revenue, coupled with Louisiana's recession triggered by the oil slump, took a hard toll across the city. As white-collar families left for work in other cities, the city lost population, dropping under a half million by 1990, more than one hundred thousand less than when my father took office, and pockets of blight reappeared.

With his sandy hair and trim mustache, David Duke, the born-again Republican, came across as a reasonable conservative, going house to house down Metairie's manicured streets, politely asking homeowners for their support. He got a boost in mid-January of 1989 when a parade in New Orleans on Martin Luther King, Jr.'s birthday turned violent, with several African Americans teenagers attacking bystanders. As police made arrests and restored order, the TV news footage sent out shock waves. Duke, who had been blaming crime on welfare recipients, began to surge in the polls.

When the primary ended, Duke had a substantial 33 percent, leading John Treen, a silver-haired stalwart of the state Republican Party, at 19 percent. John is the brother of former governor Dave Treen; he was a contractor and home builder who had long lived in Metairie. WDSU-TV reporter Clancy DuBos discovered that Duke didn't live in the district; he had taken an apartment there in time for filing. None of that seemed to deter Duke's momentum; people who wouldn't be caught dead at a Klan meeting embraced his coded message that blacks were the problem—blame the other. Treen was a lackluster campaigner who had had his share of run-ins with a number of Jefferson Parish elected officials; in any local race, you need the support of politicians who have won elections. Duke led the primary but without an absolute majority. Treen entered the runoff with a disadvantage in that sense.

The election never should have gone the way it did, but in retrospect I realize it was the shape of things to come. John Treen, an honorable man who had served in the military, distributed a four-page tabloid with parallel photographs of Treen in navy whites and Duke in a Nazi outfit at LSU; the campaign flyer also listed a number of Duke's more outrageously bigoted statements. When reporters confronted Duke for comment, he took the flyer, held it, and tore it in half, saying: "This is character assassination!" Great video—Tear up those lies! Fake news! Duke reduced damning evidence to a clever sound bite. The local media did little investigation of Duke's history with hate groups beyond calling him "a former Grand Wizard of the Ku Klux Klan." Duke's history did, though, become an issue for the Republican National Committee in Washington.

In a remarkable twist for an off-season state legislative race, President George H. W. Bush and former President Reagan endorsed John Treen—both of them clearly concerned about a hate merchant like Duke gaining an electoral platform as a newborn Republican. George W. Bush, not yet governor of Texas, made a campaign appearance for John Treen. Archbishop Philip Hannan and Loyola president Father James Carter, S.J., sent out letters expressing reservations about Duke, without actually crossing a political line to endorse Treen. African American leaders kept a muted distance, not wanting to attack Duke in a district that was 99.6 percent white, lest his counterattack make more of the issue of race than he had already done.

On election night, Duke won by 227 votes, at 50.7 percent, and the news went all over the world: former Klan Grand Wizard wins in Louisiana. At the victory party, in a Lions Club on Metairie Road, the mood was both elated and bellicose. Channel 4—WWL-TV, the CBS affiliate—dutifully ran video of a man cupping his mouth and bellowing several times, "Channel Four—*Communist!*" Cheryl and I can still recall the feeling of shock and disbelief we had as we watched the election results come in that night.

At a press conference the next day, Duke tried to put some distance between today and his long record as an anti-Semite, saying, "I have a hand of friendship out to the Jewish community." But when reporters began pressing him on the items sold by the *NAAWP News,* liked taped speeches of American Nazi Party founder George Lincoln Rockwell, he ended the conference, saying he wasn't going to "discuss what I did ten years ago."

And so David Duke came to Baton Rouge to take his seat in the legislature. He posed a huge problem for many of us who were only a year into our terms. Black caucus members were outraged by his mere presence. Democrats were stunned that someone of his ideological ilk had won.

The Republicans were in their own pickle. Duke had been a Democrat, on paper at least, until a few weeks before the election. Many Republicans saw him as a slick operator of calculated expediency, but very few wanted to speak out against him.

In those early weeks and months, all of us in the state legislature had a decision to make: attempt to work around our newly elected colleague or build a resistance and push back. Odon "Don" Bacqué, a newly elected Independent whose district included part of Lafayette, the hub city of Cajun country, researched state law and found that the statute required a candidate to be domiciled for a year in the district. I helped him circulate a copy of the statute, hoping we could have Duke removed on legal grounds. "Laws without enforcement are only empty promises," Bacqué declared. "Edmund Burke said that the only thing necessary for evil to triumph is for good men to do nothing."

The House Speaker, popular with the members, argued that

the people in Metairie had "elected Mr. Duke by a majority vote"—and therefore the people's will should be respected. He called for a vote to table Bacqué's motion, which carried 69–33. I sat there thinking about my father being threatened by Leander Perez and Willie Rainach, both long buried, and then about images of Auschwitz, the stacks of eyeglasses and suitcases of the dead, while another realization bore down on me from the comments of several colleagues—that people in their districts *liked Duke.* Others had been so mesmerized by his style as to say, "You know, he's kinda got a point. He doesn't yell and scream. He's just talking about people working, and personal responsibility, and babies not having babies—you know, an honest day's work for an honest day's pay." I heard people in the chamber mutter things like that, and kept replying, "He's not telling you what he really thinks."

Duke arrived with his agenda on the table. He was building a base by telling white people that black people were the cause of Louisiana's problems, or of their losing ground, or being poor. I began to push my colleagues, telling them, "He wants to cut programs that will help poor white people in this state—health care, education, unemployment compensation." In New York, the Anti-Defamation League began distributing a brochure called *David Duke: In His Own Words*. It showed how obsessed he was with race as biological determinism and willfully perverted history:

Jews gain certain advantages by promoting the Holocaust idea. It inspires tremendous financial aid for Israel. It makes organized Jewry almost immune from criticism. Whether the Holocaust is real or not, the Jews clearly have a motive for fostering the idea that it occurred. . . . I question whether 6 million Jews actually died in Nazi death camps. [Interview with *Hustler* magazine, reprinted in *NAAWP News,* August 1982]

In an earlier publication from the Anti-Defamation League, *David Duke: A Bigot Goes to Baton Rouge,* a fund-raising letter distributed by the NAAWP quotes Duke:

No issue is more important than our people preserving its identity, culture, and rights. An America ruled by a majority of Blacks, Mexicans and other Third World types will not be the America of our forefathers, or the kind of nation for which they struggled and sacrificed. [1986 fund-raising letter]

It sounded a whole lot like "Make America Great, Again."

A group of us decided that the most important thing we could do, short term, was make sure that not a single motion by Duke became law. We held hard to that position and won; but the battle was long, draining, and often dispiriting, just as it has been for millions of Americans appalled at Donald Trump's shameful disdain for the truth and his own bizarre behavior.

In Louisiana, we learned with Duke that demagoguery is hydra-headed, like the Greek monster with many faces and, therefore, many masks. As Michael D'Antonio reports in the biography *Never Enough,* Donald Trump in 1989 eerily echoed Duke's notion of black privilege, saying: "If I were starting off today, I would love to be a well-educated black because they have an actual advantage." With Duke, my colleagues and I

learned that you have to dig in and keep challenging a demagogue's lies; in time, truth rises with a power of its own.

On most days during a legislative session, reporters casually
follow the major bills as they move through hearings at
committees, and you'd expect to see a few of the sponsors, and
opponents, quoted in the news. Overnight, reporters from far-
away places who had never set foot in Baton Rouge showed
up to do reports on Duke. National TV interviews, with
mostly soft questions from anchors or talk-show hosts who
didn't do the hard reading about his past, allowed him to cast
himself as a maverick and a celebrity. Men and women seated
in the legislature watched this flood of attention with dread
and a certain envy. Who wouldn't want the spotlight he was
getting?

With all this free publicity, he became a kind of folk hero
overnight. Imagine what it felt like to many legislators who
lived far from the New Orleans area, watching Duke sit at his
desk in the House, opening up envelopes with checks from
people all over, and notes presumably urging him on. One
letter was simply addressed "Duke, Louisiana."

I decided to be pragmatic and establish some form of contact, regardless of our glaring moral differences, while working
resolutely to thwart his agenda. We had a conversation, and for
the first half hour or so he came off as reasonable, a guy with
a vote who might do the conventional horse-trading we all did
in getting a given measure passed into law. But as the conversation went on, his eyes ranged away from direct contact and
he started talking about the biological differences between the

races, and the need to separate the races, that blacks would be better off in other countries. It was chilling.

Again, I could not stop thinking of Auschwitz. I remembered my prayers from that day and the commitment I made to stand up against this sort of evil. *We must not let this happen again.*

Here was a closet Nazi, sowing the seeds of new bigotry in Louisiana, while soft-pedaling his repulsive record toward Jews and blacks, pulling in money from people who saw him as standing up for the underdogs.

I set out to act as a foil to the hatred of Duke and to attack his veneer of respectability. In every interview I gave, I made clear that not all white people in Louisiana or the South shared the twisted beliefs of Duke. He "doesn't care about equal rights for everybody," I told Iris Kelso of the *Times-Picayune*. "He cares about creating a white Christian nation, with no room for anybody else. He understands that if he said that stuff, he'd sound like the kook that he really is." In public meetings and at political rallies, I was more direct: "David Duke is a pathological liar."

Duke's popularity created a moral vacuum in Louisiana. Into the breach stepped an uncommon man, the Reverend James Stovall, a white Methodist minister from Baton Rouge. Jimmy Stovall saw Duke for what he was and began organizing a countermovement. Jane Buchsbaum, a New Orleans Jewish activist, joined the group, which called itself the Louisiana Coalition Against Racism and Nazism. Lance Hill, who was working on a doctorate in history at Tulane, had done research on the Klan and the NAAWP; he became director of the Louisiana Coalition. Historian Lawrence N. Powell of Tulane and New Orleans author Jason Berry also became active. But the person in the Coalition who had the most striking impact on public opinion, and on me, was Elizabeth Rickey.

A thirty-two-year-old graduate student in political science at Tulane, Beth Rickey was a member of the Republican State Central Committee. She was from Lafayette. Her father had served as an army lieutenant colonel under General George C. Patton in World War II. She was an old-school Eisenhower Republican, the kind that today's party could sorely use.

Beth Rickey and Lance Hill had done the research for John Treen's campaign flyer that Duke had torn up in front of the cameras, calling it "lies." By the time Duke won, Beth and Lance had done more extensive research on his ties to hate groups. Beth Rickey came by her party credentials through a family tradition, one that I respected. Her courage transcended politics. Interestingly, she was the niece of Branch Rickey, the president and general manager of the Brooklyn Dodgers, who integrated major-league baseball when he signed Jackie Robinson in 1947.

After Duke's victory, when she learned that he was going to Chicago to speak to a gathering of the Populist Party—the neofascist organization on whose ticket he had run for president the previous fall—Rickey jumped on a plane, went to the Chicago hotel, and giving her best Southern smile, managed to get herself past the goonlike security people carrying a hidden tape recorder. "The mood in the room was tense," she wrote later. "The speakers were all angry—angry about minorities, angry about the media, just plain angry."

An exultant Duke took the podium. "We did it!" After the explosion of applause and yells, he said: "My victory in Louisiana was a victory for the white majority movement in this country." The crowd chanted *Duke! Duke! Duke!* He continued:

"Listen, the Republican Party of Louisiana is in our camp, ladies and gentlemen. I had to run with that process, because, well, that's where our people are." As the crowd, mostly male, including skinheads and men in Klan T-shirts, thundered their approval, Beth Rickey slipped away, nervous and scared. She wanted to be out of there as quickly as possible. As Duke left the conference room, he shook hands with Art Jones, vice-chairman of the American Nazi Party, just as a television reporter closed in. Jones shoved the journalist, calling him "a low-life scumbag."

When the footage aired in Louisiana, the Republican National Committee in Washington was putting pressure on the state party to oust Duke from their fold. Duke apologized to the legislature in a statement, claiming that he had spoken to a "conservative, anti-tax" rally. But lying is like a helicopter whose wings must keep spinning to maintain altitude.

Beth Rickey was determined to show the world that David Duke was a fraud.

As we got to know each other—a Republican state committeewoman and a Democratic state representative—I found her an affable, open person who thrived on politics, yet was jittery about the drama that soon engulfed her as a party loyalist turned voice of conscience. Duke was beyond anything she had encountered before. But having seen the hatred of certain white people up close since childhood, and ever aware of that vein of anger as my life took its course, I could pick up the vibes or expressions of people who hated my father or me, and steel myself to keep moving on what I believed. Beth Rickey was getting a baptism by fire.

I used the information from Rickey and her colleague, Lance Hill, in speeches and statements; yet as I watched the groundswell build behind Duke, I knew we were in for a long haul. We all wanted to expose Duke and get his white base to see him for what he was, but his charisma and telegenic appeal, with so much TV news coverage facilitating his makeover, meant that his base was growing.

Donald Trump harvested priceless free cable coverage of his primary speeches, casting himself as the great deal maker who would restore a fallen America. Encouraging people in stadiums to beat up protesters, he projected a strongman persona. When Duke endorsed him, Trump was forced by the media to finally, if halfheartedly say, "I disavow" Duke. Did Trump's white nationalist supporters believe that? Trump cultivated the part of his base that conventional Southern conservatives would never go near, like when he said there were "good people on both sides" after the neo-Nazi violence in Charlottesville, Virginia, in which a young woman was killed by a zealot plowing through the crowd in a car.

Back in 1989, as I drove past the lush greenery along the interstate, making the eighty-mile return to New Orleans with my wife and infant daughter, I wondered what it would take before the white people who liked Duke finally saw through him. We were trying to get people to see that *the past mattered*, that Southerners long before our day had subjugated African Americans so ruthlessly, while Duke seized on embedded fears and hostility.

How do you try to course-correct history, confront the past, and change how people think? That was the root issue entwined with David Duke, who denied his past to cast himself as a newborn Republican. He did so by lying, as I said often in interviews—lying about his own past, lying about history, telling historical lies to sell books and sell himself. My father had dealt with die-hard racists as mayor. The language people used had softened in the decades since then, but as I watched a resurgent white supremacy in 1989, I wondered how bad it would get.

In May 1989 Beth visited the legislative "office" in the basement of Duke's suburban house, outside the district, which doubled as NAAWP headquarters. She purchased *The Turner Diaries,* an apocalyptic novel by a Nazi apologist about a race war, which the Anti-Defamation League called a blueprint tract by the Order, an underground terrorist group that assassinated Alan Berg, a liberal Denver talk-radio host, in 1984. Also on sale was *Hitler Was My Friend* and *The Myth of the Six Million.*

The titles of those screeds alone were offensive; the idea of hatred so organized and the politics of lying so sustained was repulsive. Yet as we know from the monitoring of hate groups by the Southern Poverty Law Center, they have surged in popularity since Donald Trump. The rise of the alt-right, with their chants of "You will not replace us" and the violence they have perpetrated, is downright scary.

After the election, Duke had marched down Metairie Road in the Jefferson Parish St. Patrick's Day parade with other officials, cheered by people on the sidewalks as a celebrity, if not a conquering hero. When the pundits and national press attacked him, Duke's base saw an underdog, a guy standing up for forgotten people. Trump cultivated a similar image, just enough to create the narrow wedge of some eighty thousand voters in the Rust Belt states who gave him a winning margin in the electoral college, despite Hillary Clinton's three-million-vote victory in the popular vote.

Riding a wave of popular support, Duke began traveling

the state, stumping against Governor Roemer's tax referendum to reduce the $700 million deficit, which had risen with the departure of two hundred thousand people during the prolonged recession. Roemer had more than a revenue revitalization plan at stake; his popularity—as a governor who took office with only 33 percent of the vote—was also riding on the outcome. Duke savaged the tax plan wherever he went. He was not the only factor, but he was a high-profile presence in its defeat, 55 percent to 45 percent.

Demagogues thrive on their own theatrics, as Duke showed in one of his most vulnerable moments. Rickey went to Baton Rouge, and in the rotunda between the House and Senate chambers, she and a colleague from Tulane handed out press releases to reporters detailing the Nazi books she had purchased from Representative Duke's office in Metairie. The state Endowment for the Humanities, in conjunction with the Simon Wiesenthal Center, had mounted an exhibition of Holocaust photographs in the rotunda. Robyn Ekings, a New Orleans WVUE-TV reporter, borrowed Beth's copy of *Did Six Million Really Die?* and waved it in front of Duke with the camera homing in. "Are you selling this book in your legislative office?" Rickey's essay, from *The Emergence of David Duke and the Politics of Race,* picks up the story:

> Duke's face reddened, and he asked her excitedly who had brought her that book. Eckings pointed at me. Duke, with obvious agitation, turned and asked why I was doing this.
>
> "You're treating me like Salman Rushdie!" he said to me, then turned on his heel and hurried away, pursued up the stairs by camera crews and reporters

until he reached the sanctity of the floor of the legislature, where the press is not allowed. This bizarre reference to the author of *The Satanic Verses,* hiding from Muslim assassins, was vintage Duke, always the martyr. Reporters told me later that Duke called his office in Metairie from the House floor and warned his staff not to sell any more books.

"The Nazi books" incident was considered a successful hit at Duke's claims that he had changed. [Republican Party] Chairman William Nungesser called to congratulate me after he saw the media coverage. However, he said that the State Central Committee should not say anything about Duke. Nungesser still clung to the idea that Duke was not a racist but just an opportunist.

The late William Nungesser maneuvered his troops to avoid censuring or ejecting Duke from the fold—he was bringing in new people, some of the Reagan Democrats, and other people from the far-right fringes who had not been active before. Beth Rickey felt betrayed, justifiably so, as Duke began gaining ground. Nungesser later told the *New Republic* that Duke was "an opportunist, rotten to the core."

Duke's statewide campaign attacking Roemer's tax referendum provided him with a network of contacts to build an organization to seek a larger base. Less than a year later, Duke took aim at the 1990 U.S. Senate race. The incumbent, J. Bennett Johnston, was a Shreveport lawyer who had originally served in the State Senate, lost the 1971 governor's race to Edwards by a whisker, and with momentum from that effort won a special election in 1972 to fill the seat of U.S. Senator

Allen Ellender, who had unexpectedly died. Johnston was a conservative Democrat with support from the oil-and-gas industry; he shifted with the times, forging ties with African American leaders. An adroit Senate tactician, Johnston knew how to pass bills and steer funds to the state for road construction and for major projects for ports, municipalities, and universities—he had a record of delivering to his constituents.

I strongly supported Johnston, and felt that I could help him generate the substantial African American vote I thought he needed to win by a large margin. The question haunting me was how far Duke's road show of demagoguery would take him—how deep his lies had penetrated, how much had public opinion shifted to his "issues"? The *Times-Picayune* assigned Tyler Bridges to cover Duke full-time. As the campaign came down to Johnston, Duke, and Ben Bagert, a Republican attorney and former state senator, Bridges reported that in the 1980s Duke celebrated Hitler's birthday each April. A former girlfriend of Duke's gave Bridges insight on his adulation of Hitler. As the Louisiana Coalition Against Racism and Nazism unearthed more information about Duke's links to neo-Nazi groups, the reporting opened a larger lens on Duke's Nazi background, which made "former Klan Wizard" a soft way of identifying him—which journalists and talk-show producers still do when he finds a way to pop up.

As Duke gained momentum, a polarizing force stoking people's fears and resentments, I knew he had his share of Teflon—the record of a Klansman and closet Nazi didn't bother his hardening base. How long would it take for the other white voters to realize that he was a fraud?

Donald Trump is not a Nazi; yet he has courted white nationalists as Duke did, and like Duke, he speaks and tweets a fountain of lies, lying as naturally as normal people try to be truthful. All the bravado and psychological projection in that gimmicky term *Fake news!* as the media report his falsehoods is a booming echo to me of Duke comparing himself to Salman Rushdie as a martyr of free speech, or tearing up the paper with details on his Nazi background, crying "Character assassination!" As we finish this book in early 2018, with indictments in the Russia investigation of Special Counsel Robert S. Mueller III and escalating political drama, I watch our country's institutional crisis provoked by Trump, and my thoughts turn again to the parallels with David Duke's psychodrama. There is nothing the country is experiencing today that we in Louisiana haven't seen or faced in the last thirty years.

As the 1990 campaign began, Senator Johnston sent pollster Geoff Garin to do a focus group of twelve white swing voters from Bossier City, next door to the senator's hometown of Shreveport. "Garin moderated the ninety-minute session and began with a few noncommittal questions to loosen them up," Tyler Bridges writes in *The Rise of David Duke.*

"What are you looking for in a senator?" he asked next.

"Someone who still stand up to the NAACP," said one man.

"The NAACP is the most powerful interest group in America," said another man.

"All the benefits go to blacks at the expense of whites," said a woman.

For nearly the rest of the session, the group poured out hostility toward blacks, or "niggers" as two of them repeatedly said—and praised Duke as willing to stand up to blacks and the political establishment. When Garin asked if anyone was concerned about Duke's Klan past, no one responded. A few minutes later, when he asked if Duke's Nazi past was of concern, one woman said, "You know, Hitler had some good ideas." As the group filed out, Garin was shaken. A veteran pollster, he had spent more than a decade directing focus groups, particularly when the topic was race. But he had never seen such anger directed at blacks or the political establishment.

Duke had aired no political spots at that point; he had gotten more national TV coverage than any Louisiana politician, and tons of coverage in state. The people in that focus group got his message. Duke pushed a bill to gut affirmative action in Louisiana, which would have thrown a wrench into contracts between the state and federal government. The bill passed the House when normally centrist Cajun legislators, bristling over the refusal of three African American colleagues to support a lottery bill, threw their votes to the Duke measure. His bill died in the Senate. Without a forceful presence by Roemer, and with Duke getting so much attention that his every move generated headlines, reactionary impulses spilled out in the legislature, reminding me of the Yeats poem with the line: "Things fall apart; the centre cannot hold." The House moved a bill that I opposed—which passed despite being transparently unconstitutional—to subject record producers to misdemeanor fines if they did not put warning labels on morally objectionable lyrics in satanic heavy metal and rap music discs sold to minors. Pleas rained down from Henry Mancini, Andy Williams, and the Neville Brothers, the Grammy-winning kings of New Orleans rock, who were on tour in London and threatened to stop performing in Louisiana if the bill passed. New Orleans entrepreneurs were trying to secure an agreement to locate a Grammy Hall of Fame in the city. As the bill moved ahead, the National Academy of Recording Arts and Sciences president Michael Greene, in Los Angeles, said that if the governor did not veto the bill, "We will pull all our initiatives out of Louisiana, as we did in Arizona when they refused to have the Martin Luther King holiday. We just won't go there." Roemer did eventually veto the bill.

Duke was gaining visibility as he ran for the Senate. Bennett Johnston began attacking the NAAWP in speeches, making Duke's past an issue; the Louisiana Committee Against Racism and Nazism aired spots on his Nazi past. The national Republican Party helped Johnston by failing to give candidate Ben Bagert—the official GOP nominee—adequate funds for a competitive campaign. Bagert dropped out near the end. Johnston was reelected in a landslide, 54 percent to 43.5 percent. But within that loss, David Duke had won nearly two out of every three white votes—a far cry from his slim 227-vote margin of victory in the Metairie district some twenty months earlier.

After two full years in the state legislature, Duke had failed to pass a single instrument as he faced increasing opposition from my colleagues in the House and Senate. I was proud of our coalition, of my colleagues who continued to stand up against Duke's agenda of bigotry, and of our democratic institutions that had successfully boxed in Duke's progress. Unbowed, Duke felt the wind at his back and decided to give up his legislative seat to run against Roemer for governor in the election of 1991. I was happy to be rid of his poisonous presence in the State House, but I knew the election would be a nightmare as he carried his message of hate across the state. Still, I saw no way for the electoral math to work in his favor.

The late John Maginnis, an able chronicler of Louisiana politics, memorably called that election "the race from hell." The governor seemed rudderless as the campaign geared up. Duke was challenging him from the hard right, and former governor Edwin Edwards was hungry for political redemption.

As governor in the 1970s, Edwards had embraced New Orleans's economic potential after the building of the Louisiana Superdome, with support for infrastructure projects and for growing the tourist economy. He got behind much of the agenda that my father, and his successor, Dutch Morial, put before the legislature in Baton Rouge, seeking support for capital improvements and programs to benefit the city. Edwards realized that New Orleans was becoming the economic engine of the state and was generally supportive.

After serving two terms in the 1970s, Edwards had been ineligible for a third consecutive one. He made a roaring comeback in 1983 against Dave Treen, the state's first Republican governor since Reconstruction, a dutiful man with moderate politics and a bland personality. In a debate, Edwards quipped, "Dave, your problem is that it takes you an hour and a half to watch *60 Minutes.*" Oil production was humming in that election when Edwards bragged to *Times-Picayune* reporter Dean Baquet (today executive editor of the *New York Times*) that he was "safe with voters unless caught in bed with a dead woman or a live boy." In promising, good times, his exotic personality demolished Treen in a landslide, and he served one term.

Now he wanted a fourth term, something no Louisiana governor had achieved, and planned to hit Roemer from the left. Edwards traveled the state in a Winnebago with his girlfriend and staffers, hammering at Roemer every chance he got.

Edwards typified Louisiana's joie de vivre culture, a witty, roguish cad with a soft Cajun accent and a loose political style you find in few other states. During that third term, Edwards was twice tried for rigging hospital contracts, but was acquitted. The economy was in free fall as the price of oil had plunged; the state budget was tied to mineral severance taxes, which meant a cutback in state services. The oil industry, a major source of state jobs, was closing offices in New Orleans and elsewhere, with a rollback of drilling jobs in the state and on offshore sites in the Gulf of Mexico. People were literally leaving their homes, dropping the house keys in night deposit boxes at the banks, driving away from their mortgages and equity, and seeking employment and new lives in other states. This was particularly hard on New Orleans, where thousands of middle-class families, including middle-class whites and upwardly mobile African Americans, left to find quality work in cities like Chicago, Houston, and Atlanta. Having dropped out of the race for a fourth term just a few years earlier, Edwards was giving it one last try.

In the 1991 gubernatorial election, David Duke made a hard pitch for Evangelical voters by proclaiming himself a pro-life Christian. The man who wanted welfare mothers to be inoculated with birth control serum, the man who had birthday parties for the worst mass murderer in European history, was suddenly a defender of life in the womb. And some Evangelical voters took the bait. When Duke knocked Roemer out of the primary, the Republicans had a nightmare. Edwin

Edwards, the Democrat they hated most, was now poised to win against Duke, their candidate by default, who was soon being savaged by TV spots of Nazi troops as his "past" became an international story.

Across the state, bumper stickers started to crop up: *Vote for the Crook. It's Important.* Many people in Louisiana who could never imagine voting for Edwards, including Republicans, realized the disaster Louisiana faced should Duke win. In the final weeks, Duke, the born-again Christian, was attacking Edwards for his religious beliefs—being pro-choice. In a state where most people did not like abortion, Edwards crushed Duke with 61 percent of the vote. The message got through, you could say. Duke, however, received nearly six hundred thousand white votes, a huge number for a man whose Nazi sympathies were finally plastered all over the media.

Within a space of several years, both Edwards and Duke would go to federal prison. Duke pleaded guilty to federal charges of filing a false tax return and mail fraud in December 2002. He served fifteen months in prison. In 2000, after it was proved that Edwards extorted nearly $3 million from companies that applied for casino licenses during his last term in office, he was convicted on seventeen counts of racketeering, mail and wire fraud, conspiracy, and money laundering. Edwards was sentenced to ten years in prison and served eight. He did not seek reelection and maintains his innocence to this day.

As Duke sank in respectability and visibility, many of us felt a long hangover from his brief time in the sun. Before the 2016 presidential campaign, I can imagine that savants of the Beltway saw Duke as an aberration, the bizarre politics of a backwater state. In fact, our nightmare was a precursor of where our country is today. In those years, Louisiana politics demonstrated the raw susceptibility of voters, particularly Evangelical Christians, who rallied behind David Duke— trailed by TV spots exposing his Nazi beliefs—as a would-be defender of human life. It is the same phenomenon that allowed Christians in 2016 to support Donald Trump, despite the women who accused him of sexually assaulting them, after the *Access Hollywood* video in which he bragged about groping women, using words that TV networks bleeped out. Have we gotten to the point where winning is everything? It is clear there is a deal with the devil, where morals, personal responsibility, or principles are secondary to election wins.

We live in an age of disinformation, with so many overloaded circuits that journalism and news gathering is part of a strange digital stratosphere with few restraints and with easily doctored images that distort reality, and where the old role of spin doctors—those who seek to turn public opinion—is fast subsumed by con artists on social media, or even Russian manipulation. This is an atmosphere in which demagogues thrive.

Back in 1990, I watched well-intentioned conservatives in our legislature buckle under to reactionary tides that surged because of Duke, even though he lacked the ability to pass any legislation. The chaos that followed as Roemer had to veto bills that had no constitutional validity made Louisiana a source of derision in the media and political life generally. David Duke was alt-right in the soft verbal currency of today; he ran on a racist, isolationist, nativist platform, and after three years, finally, sank like a stone in water. Those were hard, dark, grueling years for people who loved the state and wanted to make it better. Steve Bannon is doing the same thing to the Republican Party today. Congress is bipolar after a decade of Tea Party members pushing a radical agenda. Donald Trump's flailing inability to lead and the temper tantrums of his bizarre, hair-trigger-tweeting personality open a window for the likes of Bannon to slither through. The nativist, isolationist agenda Bannon and Breitbart are pushing has the face of white supremacy leering at every turn at the party once led by Eisenhower, a war hero, and Abraham Lincoln.

We saw it all coming in Louisiana years ago. When people are scared and hurting, when the jobs are drying up and they get angry, and a demagogue arises pointing the finger at black people and brown people—blame the other—it takes a counteroffensive not just to expose the lies but to offer people hope and a belief in the better impulses of democracy. When the truth is lost, the battle to fill that vacuum is a sinister spectacle and a struggle from which good people can never call retreat. From our days with Duke, I can tell you how to end it. You have to confront those tactics straight up, shine a bright light on them, and reveal the truth. And then you must confront the bigotry behind them head-on, stay on course, and pull the tree up from the root. There is no other way forward.

CHAPTER 4

Politics in Disaster Time

In 1960, the year I was born, my grandmother Loretta
Landrieu paid fifteen thousand dollars for a patch of land
along Lake Pontchartrain, about thirty miles out from New
Orleans, near the town of Slidell. That "camp," which was a
small house that looked like a triple-wide trailer, had a long
wooden pier that jutted out into the saltwater lake. By the early
1970s we were nineteen kids in all, counting the ten children
of my aunt and uncle. We grew up swimming and skiing on
the lake, as well as playing baseball, football, and volleyball on
the grass. We would fish off the pier with cane poles. My
grandfather Joe Landrieu hovered like a sheepdog, watching
each of us with an eye that didn't miss a lick. As soon as someone caught a fish, usually a croaker or catfish (or, God forbid,
a stingray), the gaggle of us exploded in excitement—poles
clattering, fish lines flying about. And as we circled the trium-
phant one gripping the pole with that fish on the hook, amid
a mess of lines piled on the pier, "Paw Paw," someone would
call, "my line is tangled!"

Most people would look at a ball of twisted fishing line, clear it away, and start anew. Not my grandpa. He would sit there stoically, sometimes thirty minutes at a time, and methodically untangle the clump. He wasted nothing. I never heard him yell or curse; he rebaited our hooks and put us back in place on the pier, making sure that we held our cane poles—until someone caught the next fish and our tiny world broke into squeals and excitement all over again. As time went on and my grandparents passed away and the children became adults with children of their own, my father bought out my uncle's share of the place. He and my mother would never dream of leaving the house where we grew up on South Prieur Street; but they relished the time at the lakeside camp, where the gradual addition of rooms could accommodate the growing number of grandchildren, though not all thirty-eight at once. To this day, the camp holds our family together.

In 2002, it had been fifteen years since my election to the State House, which met a few months a year and was not full-time work. I had built a solid business with a solo law practice. That year, I traveled the state stumping for U.S. Senator Mary Landrieu in her campaign for a second term. Mary had a tough race against Republican opponent Suzie Haik Terrell. President George W. Bush and Vice President Dick Cheney, former President George H. W. Bush and Barbara Bush, and Bob Dole and Rudy Giuliani all campaigned for Terrell. They wanted that seat for a 52-vote GOP majority. Mary won the race by carrying Acadiana, sugarcane country, attacking Bush's support for the Central American Free Trade Agreement, a move that augured steep losses for growers and Louisiana's farm sector. In a state tilting red, she was reelected by forty thousand votes.

I was forty-three and ready to move beyond the legislature.

The gubernatorial election of 2003 drew a crowded field on the Democratic and Republican sides. I sought the lieutenant governor's seat, which had been a springboard to higher positions for previous holders. A former lieutenant governor, Melinda Schwegmann, whose husband owned a New Orleans–area supermarket chain, and former congressman Clyde Holloway, both Republicans, entered the race, as well as a few others.

I traveled the state calling for a strategy to attract more business and boost tourism, the office's major function. I wanted to bring people together and spoke openly of embracing the New South, with diversity a strength as we came together across the lines that once divided us. My rhetoric was not earth shattering, but in the dozen years since the Duke nightmare I wasn't sure how many whites had turned a corner, so to speak. Nor did I grasp how difficult it would be to achieve the agenda, in light of events that lay ahead. Nevertheless, the campaign message resonated, despite some rooted resentment about my father's role in integrating New Orleans. I won the primary with 53 percent, hence no runoff—a rarity in a state where Democratic officials kept migrating to the Republican Party. I carried most of the sixty-four parishes and won 80 percent of the vote in my home parish of Orleans.

The lieutenant governor manages the Department of Culture, Recreation and Tourism, which also has an appointed secretary. You can also do whatever is assigned by the governor, but the tourism duties give a certain degree of self-definition. I embraced growing the "cultural economy." Tourism and culture was one of the largest employment sectors in the state.

As a onetime struggling actor, I knew that the contributions made by back-of-the-house workers—from set designers and sound techs to photographers and makeup artists—made a real difference. We implemented a grant program for creative people on a range of projects that was designed to get funds directly into the cultural economy without layers of bureaucracy. I saw creative people—directors, writers, painters, sculptors, and folk artists—as the backbone of the glitzy tourism industry. New Orleans had 130 art galleries, one of the highest number per capita of any city. A grant of several thousand dollars made a difference to an artist needing supplies to create works for an exhibition.

Early in my term I began streamlining how the department functioned, while expanding its mission. In my campaign travels I had been struck by the beauty and history of Louisiana; I was also disappointed by the lack of diversity in what we honored in our parks, museums, and cultural spaces. For all of the achievements of African Americans, we had little to show for that formally. I appointed the first African American assistant secretary of tourism, Chuck Morse. We knew that securing legislative funds for an entire new museum would be a stretch, so we decided to consider the state as a living museum and created the African American Heritage Trail, promoting and explaining important destinations and learning experiences from New Orleans to Shreveport and in between, sites like churches, gravesites, museums, and plantations. Later, we created a marketing fund dedicated to attracting African American visitors. We put a huge focus on promoting growing major events, from the Essence Music Festival to the Bayou Classic to the New Orleans Jazz & Heritage Festival. These efforts solidified Louisiana as the number-one destination for African Americans in the country.

But the office I won was soon hit by a force that none of my staff or I could have imagined.

On August 27, 2005, a Saturday, I sat in Lawless Memorial Chapel at Dillard University for the funeral of Clarence Barney, the longtime leader of the Urban League in New Orleans. Marc Morial, Dutch's son, who had served eight years as mayor of New Orleans before becoming president of the National Urban League in New York, sat next to me. Both of us worried about the news of a massive storm building in the Gulf of Mexico. Hurricane Katrina was growing in scope and intensity more than any storm we had ever seen. Mayor C. Ray Nagin and Governor Kathleen Blanco were discussing whether to order a mass evacuation. That would mean a huge allocation of state and local resources for first responders and public shelters. Many people weren't waiting to be told to leave. By Saturday afternoon a record outflow of vehicles from the metropolitan area, including Jefferson, St. Bernard, and low-lying Plaquemines parishes, had caused gridlock on the highways headed east, west, and north. Everyone was racing away from the monster gaining force in the Gulf.

At four in the morning on Sunday, August 28, Cheryl and I gathered the five children and headed west to Baton Rouge; a drive that typically took ninety minutes became a seven-hour bumper-to-bumper grind. Gracie was in her senior year at Dominican, where Emily was a junior. Matt was a freshman at Jesuit; Benjamin was in middle school at Christian Brothers, and Will was in grade school at Lusher, a public school. Like everyone else in emergency mode, we assumed that a few days after the hurricane passed, we'd head home, like we always did.

On Sunday, Mayor Nagin and Governor Blanco called for mandatory evacuation, the first ever for New Orleans. When

I got to the Emergency Operations Center in Baton Rouge and saw the staggering size of the storm on computer models and National Weather Service data, I telephoned my parents, who were still at home in New Orleans. I asked my father what they were planning.

"We're going to ride it out. Son, you know, we've been through this many times."

"Look, Dad, you've gotta go."

"Son, we're not leaving."

"Would you put Momma on the phone?"

My mother came on. "I'm at the Emergency Operations Center, Mom. I'm looking at this storm." I told her it was worse than Hurricane Betsy in 1965—which flooded a huge area of the Lower Ninth Ward, killing 81 people in Louisiana. I said it was going to be more severe than Hurricane Camille in 1969—which had killed 259 people in the Gulf South and hit the Mississippi coast like a sledgehammer, splintering beach-front homes and businesses.

"Oh, honey, we're really thinking about staying."

"Mom, this is your lieutenant governor speaking, and I am basically ordering you to leave because you're going to get killed!"

"Well, son, you tell that lieutenant governor it's *none of his business!*"

We didn't get very far after that. With events converging around me, I called a sibling to echo my message and had to let it go.

The Emergency Operation Center was what I imagined the White House Situation Room to be in times of crisis. Governor Blanco and her key advisers, various department heads, and officials of the State Police and National Guard were hunkered down. We were going to have to open the Superdome as a shelter of last resort. There's an irony here that's often missed. The vast damage caused by Hurricane Katrina and the flooding after the levees broke left enduring images of catastrophe, but with 1.5 million people leaving the greater New Orleans area over a two-day period, despite the traffic, the Katrina evacuation was the most successful in American history. Imagine how much worse the human suffering would have been had most of those people stayed.

Hurricane Katrina was a disaster unlike anything Americans had ever seen in real time, on television. The flooding exposed a global audience to epic damage, great suffering, and a breakdown in government operations without precedent in recent American history. We also saw uncommon heroism and resilience as people did their best to help others. But for all of the striving to restore togetherness in times of crisis, there is a deeper, more difficult story to Katrina that also tells us about America as a nation. It is not a story about coming together to face all obstacles, when goodness prevails. It is a coming-apart story. The underbelly of it all.

In 2005, the overriding concern by many hurricane experts was that a storm path would swirl upriver from the Gulf along the Mississippi, producing a funnel, spilling waves over the river levees and causing widespread flooding. Katrina took a different route. Pushing east of the mouth of the Mississippi, the winds sent a mammoth sheet of water toward eastern New Orleans over fragile wetlands interlaced with thousands of canals carved for offshore oil production. One side of that large lane straddled a levee along the Gulf Intracoastal Waterway;

the other levee shouldered the Mississippi River-Gulf Outlet (MR-GO). Katrina did not hit the Mississippi River but swept across that denuded area between the Intracoastal and the MR-GO as if it were a bowling alley, a giant water wall barreling toward the city. It was those canal levees that gave way, not the river's.

Environmentalists had long decried the shredding of the wetlands, a coastal forest and hurricane buffer of yesteryear. One man I knew well had railed against MR-GO for years—Henry "Junior" Rodriguez, the St. Bernard Parish president. A descendant of eighteenth-century Spanish settlers called Los Isleños, who once inhabited islands in the lakes south of the city, Junior Rodriguez is massive presence at three hundred pounds. With a silver mane and a fondness for cowboy boots, Junior is a native son of an area where many families rely on commercial fishing, or earn their livelihoods on the river or in the oil industry. Junior Rodriguez is a force of nature. To say that he hated MR-GO, dug through coastal wetlands in his political territory, is a huge understatement; he shouted about it to anyone who would listen. He said other things I prefer not to put in a book. Building MR-GO destroyed twenty thousand acres of marshland as the Army Corps of Engineers dredged an artery five hundred feet wide to create a shipping channel to move cargo from the Mississippi River to the Gulf. It was finished in 1963.

In 2001, Christopher Hallowell published *Holding Back the Sea*, a prescient book on the crisis of Louisiana's wetlands: "Erosion from ships and storms has gouged it 2,000 feet wide and made it a freeway to New Orleans for any hurricane that happens to come from the right direction," wrote Hallowell.

"The surrounding marsh, now vulnerable to storms and salt water, has all but died . . . along with 40,000 acres of mature cypress trees. Now, storm surges can invade the marsh through the straight-arrow channel and smash into New Orleans." That is exactly part of what happened with Hurricane Katrina.

As I stood in the operations center in Baton Rouge, calling officials, allies, and friends across the southern parishes, Junior Rodriguez was on my mind. His cell didn't answer. The levees, we learned later from federal investigations, had been compromised through faulty design and maintenance by the Army Corps of Engineers. Since then, the levees have had a major $14.6 billion upgrade. Yet even today, if you know that a mammoth storm is heading toward the New Orleans area, the smart thing to do is go far away as fast as you can.

I was in regular contact that Sunday with Doug Thornton, the manager of the Louisiana Superdome, and officials in parishes near New Orleans. The Superdome had taken in twenty-five thousand people—for the most part, poor people who had no cars or means to leave. And it was bad in there. In my last call to Thornton at about 2:00 A.M. on Monday morning, he yelled over the din, "*It's really bad in here!* Water's coming in from the roof!" Then the phone went dead.

I finally got through to Junior Rodriguez in Chalmette, the parish seat of St. Bernard. He was on the second floor of the municipal complex, the first floor was under water, and he was nervous. "The water is rising. We don't know how far it's going to get." Junior's phone went dead.

I caught a few hours of sleep overnight in the Emergency Operations Center. On Monday, we got word from General Bennett Landreneau of the Louisiana National Guard that the storm surge from the Gulf had crashed into the St. Bernard Parish levee.

On Tuesday, the day after Katrina hit, I went into New Orleans with Department of Wildlife and Fisheries first responders—tough, capable people who knew how to navigate rivers. They had boats, which were crucial. We headed toward New Orleans from Baton Rouge on I-10, and on passing Louis Armstrong airport, began to see downed power lines and cars sitting on the side of the interstate as people waited for rescue. We had to snake along River Road to get from Jefferson Parish into the city, and as we made our way onto Magazine Street, with the zoo on our right and Audubon Park on our left, the city had the eerie silence of a ghost town. Over the next few days, as we drove back and forth from Baton Rouge to get boats into flooded neighborhoods and pull people to safety, the city I adored for its greenery had turned upside down—there were branches and upended roots everywhere. And it had an awful stench. You drive through your day and take sounds for granted—birds warbling, cars chugging, children yelling at play. New Orleans was brown and still, as if a bomb had hit, shutting off sound.

We made it downtown to the Superdome, where I had memories of Saints games, concerts, and extravaganzas during Carnival season. Now people were bunched on the sidewalks out front, trying to escape the heat and miserable conditions in the Dome. Doug Thornton gave me a list of immediate needs—water, ice, food, and transportation to carry people stuck in that fetid environment out of the flooded city, out to someplace else. I jotted down the things he needed and kept moving.

Because of Louisiana's history of hurricanes and flooding, I had long been interested in emergency response mechanisms, how to connect on-the-ground assets with the highest reaches of government. Trivial as it may seem, you need a clear command and control, clear coordination, and clear communication. I needed to get solid information back to the EOC in Baton Rouge. But because cell towers were down, there were no communications with Baton Rouge until I could get back physically. Five years later, when I became mayor of New Orleans, I was obsessed with coordinating City Hall and law enforcement on crowd control, given the major ball games and entertainment events we have throughout the year—and even more so in advance of storms. The wave of mass shootings had not hit New Orleans in 2005, though when it did we made policy changes with the police. Not a day goes by that my team doesn't hear me talk about downline logistics, that the weakest link will destroy the best strategy. Without a stable line of communications, you invite failure.

When you see the city you love so wounded, your first thought is to rescue as many people as you possibly can. But on leaving the Superdome we had to go next door to the Hyatt Regency hotel, behind City Hall, to meet with Mayor Ray Nagin and coordinate with the city. The mayor and Governor Blanco were very different personalities; it was no secret that they got along poorly. She was a former teacher, legislator, and hands-on veteran of state government; he had been a cable company executive with a background in sales. Blessed with charm and a natural charisma, Nagin vaulted into office with no experience in governing, nor in getting along with officials you may not like. In politics you have to deal with people you do not like if you want to deliver for the common good. I had gotten along well enough with Nagin, but when I found him on an upper floor of the hotel, I became concerned.

"What do you need?" I said.

He sat in a chair, unable to focus. *He seems out of it,* I thought. Standing in the Hyatt Regency room with Nagin, I knew we had work to do. The city had a bus fleet for evacuation needs. "Where are the buses?" I asked.

"We don't have the keys," he said. I had not yet seen TV footage of the city's bus fleet engulfed by the flood, or learned what went wrong in that chain of command.

I spoke to one of his staffers. "I'm here on behalf of the governor. Figure out what you need and let us know."

Rumors abounded in the chaos of those first few days; there was widespread talk of looting, and a report that some thieves had broken into an Uptown drugstore, shuttered after the storm. The New Orleans Police Department communications system was broken. Hospitals were on high alert to guard their pharmacies. Nagin's rhetoric cast himself as a victim of politics and a city beleaguered by addicts "probably" with guns. We now know this was not the case.

"Many of the more toxic rumors seem to have come from evacuees, half-crazed with fear sitting through night after night in the dark," David Carr wrote in the *New York Times* on September 19, 2005. "Victims, officials and reporters all took one of the most horrific events in American history and made it worse than it actually was."

We drove through the French Quarter and onto St. Claude Avenue, heading into the Ninth Ward, where we knew the flood situation was dire; it's one of the lowest parts of a city already below sea level. The Wildlife and Fisheries agents were waiting with boats after we crossed the St. Claude Bridge over the Industrial Canal into the Lower Ninth Ward. Water was so high people were stranded on rooftops. We set out in boats, helping people out of the flooded houses, getting them to high ground. I couldn't stop thinking about Junior Rodriguez and his people to the south, in St. Bernard Parish. With the Wildlife and Fisheries agents doing rescue work, and volunteers from the "Cajun Navy" arriving with their own vessels and magnificent bravado, I took a boat and started navigating down the flooded road, about three miles to the St. Bernard Parish government complex in Chalmette. It was surrounded by water. I made it onto the second floor, where traumatized officials had spent the worst night of their lives. The heat was severe. Junior Rodriguez was like the boxer played by Robert De Niro in *Raging Bull,* sopping wet in his underwear, the silver hair in dank curls, his jowls dripping. State Representative Nita Hutter and several other officials were there as well. I pulled Junior aside. "I'm here for the governor. What do you need?"

"The whole parish is destroyed," he said in a ragged voice. Word had come of thirty-five people drowned in a nursing home. "Mitch, I need water, food, and dynamite."

"Dynamite?"

I think Junior Rodriguez wanted to blow a hole in a levee to discharge water out of the flooded area, back into the Mississippi.

"Junior, I'm not asking the governor for dynamite."

Creating a hole in an already compromised levee struck me as dangerous, but I suspected where he'd gotten the idea. During the Great Mississippi Flood of 1927, the New Orleans business elite persuaded the governor and federal authorities to dynamite levees downriver, intentionally flooding St. Bernard

Parish in order to spare the city from inundation. The move, which proved to be unnecessary, caused massive damage to low-lying farms and towns, as John M. Barry chronicled in *Rising Tide*, a celebrated history.

> New Orleans meanwhile was enjoying itself. The fine families, as if on a picnic, traveled down to see the great explosion that would send dirt hundreds of feet high and create a sudden Niagara Falls. Cars jammed the road down to St. Bernard, and yachts crowded the river.
>
> But not just anyone could witness the explosion. The men who had decided to dynamite the levee controlled those permits. Residents of St. Bernard could not witness the destruction of the levee, of their parish.

Junior Rodriguez was a friend, and in the steaming despair after what he and his colleagues had endured, I kept the focus on getting a supply line for immediate needs like water, food, and rescue. I wanted to do more, but the hideous reality I learned that week is that in a time of crisis, you can only do what you have the capacity to do, and there were thousands of Juniors in desperate straits. My job was to get accurate information to the EOC, and then go help the people I found in immediate need. Junior could have left, caught a ride with me to the Hyatt or a cool place in Baton Rouge; he stayed. I made trips back to the Lower Nine and St. Bernard every day that week.

As the sight of people trapped on rooftops of the Lower Ninth Ward became a recurrent image in TV coverage, I heard

African Americans fume that whites had dynamited the Industrial Canal floodwall, causing people to drown in the haunting, apocalyptic scenes captured on our screens. There was no evidence of this: in fact, a barge had crashed through the canal floodwall, sending off a loud sound like a thunderclap before the oily waters rushed in. And in those early days, several places in St. Bernard caught fire, with booming explosions. People in the Lower Nine had heard of the dynamiting of the levees in 1927—a major news event back then, part of the memory passed from one generation to the next. Some African Americans in the poorest part of the city seized on the idea of a white conspiracy during that achingly slow federal rescue in 2005.

On Monday night I got back to Baton Rouge and went to check on Cheryl and the children. More people had arrived—two of Cheryl's sisters, other family members and their children, and a couple of dogs. As TV news showed that the levees had buckled and the city was filling with water, I figured that my parents' house on South Prieur Street had flooded, learning much later that it had taken some seven feet of water. My sister Madeleine and her husband, attorney Paige Sensenbrenner, lost their home in Lakeview; my brother Martin had his Lakeview home inundated by the flood. Some days later, Cheryl and I learned that floodwater under our house Uptown had caused the downstairs floor to warp, and a pine tree had fallen on our roof, causing rainfall flooding upstairs. It took many months of dealing with adjusters and contractors before we got back in the house. Ours was a fairly typical experience for an extended New Orleans family. The storm spared no one.

And by Tuesday no one had heard from my mother or father.

The breakdown in FEMA's response is now infamous, and it had a crippling impact on President George W. Bush's standing, but all sorts of people did come to New Orleans in our darkest hour, people arriving from far-off places to help when help was needed most. As I shuttled back and forth to Baton Rouge, visiting my family, relaying information and supplies to the governor and people in the EOC, stocking our vehicles with water, food, emergency items, and then heading back to New Orleans, the ordeal of getting people into dry places showed me human decency at its fullest.

A big guy with a ruddy face was cooking on a grill outside of Harrah's casino on Poydras Street downtown. The police and National Guard were blocking people from getting into the city because of the pressure to evacuate those stranded in the Superdome and another emergency shelter, the Ernest N. Morial Convention Center, which had become horror shows in news coverage. The city would be off-limits for weeks as the floodwaters slowly drained. Entergy, the public utility, would work crews through the night to get the city back on the grid, street by darkened street, for months afterward.

I introduced myself to the man with the grill. "What are you doing?"

"*God called me to come!* I'm from Daphne, Alabama, and I'm cooking for whoever is hungry."

"Good for you! Keep cooking!"

The next day he had two grills, barbecuing away, first responders and nomads waiting in line with paper plates. He waved me over. "Now look, Lieutenant Governor, I've got trucks of food coming from Alabama and the State Police wanna stop 'em." He had found a way to get contraband food into the city and feed people. We cut through red tape to keep him cooking; he wound up with four grills outside his Winnebago, feeding thousands in those awful days.

My siblings and I were frantic to find my parents, calling people across the state, when my sister Melanie, who lives in Mandeville, just across Lake Pontchartrain, located them in Crystal Springs, Mississippi. They were at Tiny's house. "Tiny is a lady who was a barmaid for Mr. Sam Albano, a friend of my daddy's who had a bar and my daddy was his lawyer," Melanie told *Newsweek*. "She'd been calling them to come and visit, so that's where they went."

Realizing it would be months before their water-battered house on Prieur Street could be restored, my parents bought a small boathouse on the Tchefuncte River in St. Tammany Parish, across Lake Pontchartrain. They eventually got the Prieur Street house rebuilt and returned to live there. Cheryl and I, meanwhile, got the children situated in Baton Rouge schools for the fall semester, with a hectic transportation schedule in the weeks to come. At least we were all safe, and together.

The rescue work I did in the boats we hauled from Baton Rouge was a bone-chilling experience, but what sticks in my mind are those examples of pluck and wit from African American residents in the Lower Ninth Ward. As we maneuvered through water up to our windshields, people called from balconies and rooftops. You pull up to a duplex where twenty-five people are sun parched and desperate, and you only have room for fourteen in the boat. The people who cannot walk get priority; others lay them on sheets, carry them into the vessel, and go back inside. You promise to come back. They wait, we return.

At one house, near the gaping hole in the Industrial Canal floodwall, a man stood at the second-floor window as our boat pulled up. He was in his T-shirt and underwear.

"Do you want to be rescued, sir?"

"You the lieutenant governor?"

"Yes, sir."

"The lieutenant governor going to rescue me?"

"Yes, sir. But can I ask a question?"

"Sure."

"Did you hear the mayor and governor say to evacuate?"

"Yep."

"Did you hear us tell you the storm was coming?"

"Yes, sir."

"Then why are you here?"

"We don't believe anything you politicians say."

"You believe me now?"

"Well, I'm coming!"

If an epic disaster teaches a politician humility, the other end of the learning curve is a hands-on experience in getting government to deliver for people when they need it. Working with first responders showed me a spiritual magic that caused our self-made divisions to dissolve in time of crisis. Nobody cared who was driving the boat or riding. No one was concerned about whether people in the boat were black or white, rich or poor, who was from New Orleans or who was not. We had a common enemy and a common solution: we had to help people get to a better place, which gave poignant meaning to the phrase "We are all in the same boat."

I'm convinced that most of us in elective office have a basic belief in how government should best serve the people, even those who don't vote for you. Nothing levels the ideological differences like a natural disaster, which forces people to pull together. In that massive outflow of people from the New Orleans metro area, Baton Rouge, which had been smaller than New Orleans before Katrina, more than doubled in population to some eight hundred thousand in a matter of days. This put a huge strain on the resources of Mayor Kip Holden, a friend of mine from our years in the legislature. One night, after I had driven back to the operations center, Andy Kopplin, the chief of staff for Governor Blanco, grabbed me in the hallway and asked if I would intervene with Mayor Holden and State Senator Cleo Fields of Baton Rouge to allow five busloads of New Orleans citizens to stay in a park facility. Holden didn't want more people in the crowded space, said Kopplin. Fields was demanding that Holden let the buses unload there. Holden and Fields were both strong willed and not close allies.

"Can I exercise the full authority of the governor in this?" I asked Kopplin.

"Yes."

Holden was dealing with a crisis of massive overcrowding and took the position that he could not accommodate more people. I went to the back of the EOC and found General Landreneau of the Louisiana National Guard, a career military man who had made forceful TV spots denouncing David Duke as a Nazi in 1991. "General, do you have five guys to drive buses?"

"I will go get them."

He got the men out of sleep, brought them to me, and said, "Do whatever the lieutenant governor tells you."

The five guardsmen and I drove across the river to West Baton Rouge and connected with the sheriff, Mike Cazes. When the caravan from New Orleans arrived, the people in the buses were tired, wet, hungry, and homeless since the flood. Cazes provided them with bologna sandwiches and potato chips. Small hitch: It turned out that none of the five National Guardsmen had experience driving buses. Neither did I. The exhausted bus drivers had come through hours of bumper-to-bumper traffic, and though they were too tired to go on, they didn't want to surrender the keys to the vehicles—no doubt for insurance reasons.

"On the authority of the State of Louisiana," I said, "give me the keys."

The men looked at one another, looked at the National Guardsmen, and handed them over.

"Now, we need lessons in how to operate the vehicles."

We eventually loaded the people back into the buses and headed across the Mississippi River bridge along I-10 going west away from Baton Rouge and into Cajun country. An hour later we reached Lafayette in time to put all the people on a train to Houston, where the Astrodome had become a shelter for people displaced by Katrina. Soon thereafter, I flew to Houston and met up with Governor Blanco to visit the people we had evacuated, and many others living on cots in the Astrodome. The officials in Houston, led by Mayor Bill White and Harris County Judge Robert Eckels, helped us greatly, which we will long remember and will be forever grateful.

As Katrina evacuees headed off to Atlanta, Nashville, Denver, New York, and everywhere in between, the state established an emergency contact system, trying to collect as many names, cell numbers, and e-mails of displaced people as possible. The staff at my office cast lines across a broad geographic area to help people connect with FEMA for emergency help, and allow us to go and physically meet with as many people as the governor, I, and other state officials could, in order to help them begin to make their way back home. People were also locating friends on Craigslist, newsletter lists like *The New Orleans Agenda*, and through the *Times-Picayune* Web site.

When pictures hit the airwaves of thousands of poor people, mostly African Americans, huddled at the Superdome or the Convention Center or walking through water, stranded, abandoned, wet, hot, hungry, thirsty—the nation suddenly found a mirror, and we did not like what we saw. How could there still be such poverty and desperation—in America the superpower? The country was hit with a shock like the one on 9/11. Most people could not imagine that so many poor people *lived* in rocking, good-times New Orleans, or that they had no means of transportation to escape a flood. They had always been in plain sight, in some ways like the Confederate monuments we walked and drove past every day. Always there, rarely noticed. Now, in full view, those desperate souls were impossible to ignore—a legacy of the racially driven politics that controlled the city long before the civil rights era. The War on Poverty, so derided by the right, had lasted barely more than a decade, whereas a century had passed between the Civil War and the civil rights movement, a century of disenfranchisement, political and economic. You cannot undo the legacy of enforced poverty in the blink of history's eye. New Orleans did not have a public high school for African Americans until 1917. We have made great strides since then, but the city in 2005 had a poverty level of nearly

30 percent and a poorly funded social safety net. The building of a just, equitable society takes honesty, determination, and grit to withstand the reactionary forces.

It is true that Katrina in many ways did not discriminate. It hit white, black, rich, poor, old, and young. The water was high in many affluent neighborhoods. But Lieutenant General Russel Honoré, who led the military troops that stabilized the city, said it best: "Who is affected more when it's cold? Poor people. Who is affected more when it's hot? Poor people. Who is affected more when it's wet? Poor people. Who is most affected when the economy is bad? Poor people. Poor people are the most fragile." And in New Orleans, most of the people who were poor were also African American.

Long ago, the Ninth Ward housed plantations that stretched from the Mississippi River to the lake. After the Civil War, desperate to find land and housing, poor immigrants and formerly enslaved African Americans began moving to the area in the 1870s. Because of its topography, they risked flooding and other troubles to move there. It wasn't until the 1920s that there became an "upper" and "lower" Ninth Ward, divided by the Industrial Canal, which was dredged to assist the port in shipping. The Lower Ninth Ward then became even more segregated from the rest of the city. By the time Hurricane Katrina struck, it was nearly 100 percent African American.

Katrina gave the Lower Ninth Ward, nearly 100 percent black, and Lakeview, which was over 90 percent white, a water beating of equal proportion—upward of fifteen feet in both areas. Twelve years later, Lakeview has recovered, buoyantly so. It's at its highest property values and lowest crime rate, and is back bigger and stronger than ever before by nearly any measure. The Lower Ninth Ward is one of only two neighborhoods with less than 50 percent of its pre-Katrina population—a haunting shadow of what it was before. It had been a vast working-class area before the storm. Sicilians and other white ethnic groups were part of the social quilt until the 1960s, when the school desegregation crisis caused many white families to leave, some of them going over the city line into St. Bernard Parish. As the Lower Nine became more African American, the area weathered the crack epidemic that hit many inner-city enclaves in the late 1980s, with drug gangs seeking a foothold. Ironically, the level of home ownership in the Lower Ninth was remarkably high, near 60 percent.

Poor folk lived in homes whose mortgages had long been paid, but no one covered the insurance. Many did not have the money to open probate or successions; the homes were passed down through families without legal documentation. Though the storm did not discriminate in whom it hit or hurt, the ability of a person to bounce back, heal, or rebuild was determined by one's strength or vulnerability at the time of impact. Should we fault the people in the Lower Nine who neglected house insurance? I would raise another question: Should the government deny people repair costs from a federal levee failure because proof of ownership does not meet a banking standard? If people can prove that they lived in a house that was theirs, shouldn't that count? We shouldn't blame poor people for losing what they had, when the levees broke and destroyed their homes because of massive human error by the Army Corps of Engineers, a federal agency.

Angela Glover Blackwell, the founder and CEO of Policy-Link, has written that because of Katrina, "America was forced to recognize that, for Black America, far too little has changed since the civil rights struggles of the 1960s. Despite antipoverty efforts, our nation had not addressed the fundamental factors that keep people poor. To lift people out of poverty and make good on the promise of opportunity for all, we must honestly and authentically confront our nation's deepest fissure and most entrenched barrier to equity: race."

Blaming the poor for their poverty shows an America with a warped soul. The legacy of poverty is hardest for people struggling to get out of it. In New Orleans, the rooted underclass turns on a legacy of racial discrimination as it does in parts of many other cities—Detroit, Chicago, Los Angeles, and Houston, to name a few. But when the chips are down and we face a common threat, Americans work together across all lines that separate us, and surprise ourselves with how alike we are. And we need to do more of that. What we need is a political consensus to provide pathways to learning and earning for those who are poor but willing to do the hard work.

The most powerful message driven home by Katrina was one that seemed to surprise people I met outside New Orleans: the fierce determination of people who wanted to go back to neighborhoods that had been trashed by the flood. The richest and the poorest people both had families, roots, and lives that celebrate the seasons with parades, festivals, and food. The homes of the poorest were gone, but why would they *not* want to return to their city? For all of the poverty, they wanted the only lives they knew.

Riding in those boats, helping people get out, I saw women and men holding garbage bags stuffed with whatever they could carry. In that blistering heat, most people wore T-shirts; we saw people floating by in tire tubes, pawing the water without oars, fleeing for their lives. At one apartment building we reached, a little lady was holding a clock. Helping her onto the boat, I said, "Ma'am, what you doing with that clock?"

"Mitch, baby, I done lost everything. I don't know what I'm gonna do. I don't know where I'm going. But I know one thing . . ." Her voice trailed off.

"Well, what is that, ma'am?"

"I know what time it is."

She was holding on to that one piece of the place she had lost. I have mentioned that lady in countless speeches in saying why, in recovery, we cannot hold on to things. We have to let go and we can't build back the same way we were before. We have to build a city for the future. Several years ago, we were cutting the ribbon for a renovated CVS pharmacy on St. Claude Avenue in the Lower Ninth, a neighborhood slowly coming back. By this time I was no longer lieutenant governor. I was the mayor now, I was rebuilding the city, putting resources that I could allocate into the Lower Ninth, which some people even today are willing to write off. I was in the middle of a press conference when I heard somebody yelling from the back of the media, "I got something to say! I got something to say!"

This is New Orleans, where drama lurks at every turn. A woman walked up to the podium and said, "*I'm the clock lady!*" I got choked up on the spot. This woman was seared into my memory. She said her name, Margie Shorty. She'd been in Philadelphia for ten years, and just moved back. "I live around the corner!" Right near where she used to live. We hugged.

I am still haunted by those days a dozen years ago, the memories of an abandoned city, and the eerie silence broken by the cries of people trapped by the rising water, waving tattered sheets from the rooftops, yelling, "*We are still alive.*"

Tented emergency rooms hastily erected in the shadow of the Convention Center. Makeshift beds on the Superdome floor, people wet and close, children crying, hope fading. Three thousand souls stuck in a sweltering shed in the Port of St. Bernard, waiting. . . . People like apparitions emerging from the water, defiant, heads rising, then shoulders, the full person holding a black garbage bag. Some people made it out. Vera Smith lay dead on the corner of Magazine Street and Jackson Avenue. For days the street was where she lay, a thin, white sheet shrouding her frail body, a simple epitaph written in black permanent marker: "Here lies Vera. God help us." Grandmas and grandpas died in storm-battered hospitals and nursing homes. They were left on cots in a crowded chapel that became a substitute morgue. Each year, we pray at the tombs of the eighty-five bodies that to this day lay unclaimed in the Hurricane Katrina Memorial. These fathers and mothers, brothers and sisters, friends and neighbors died as our city was torn apart.

In those four horrific days, there was anarchy in the streets. And yet we found salvation, light, and hope from the angels among us. There were so many. I saw young black boys—whom some might have dismissed as the stereotype of criminal youth—pushing an old white man in a rusted wheelchair, to find water. I saw an old white woman hold the hand of a crying black girl who had lost her mother. I met a minister from Dallas who sneaked into the city to feed people; and strangers, pressed together by circumstance, leaning on one another for comfort and support.

Our inundated homes were tattooed with Xs by National Guard soldiers who went house to house to identify who was inside, living or dead. Many people had to gut their houses to the bone. Three feet of water on the second floor; mud caked everywhere; the unforgettable stench of a rotten refrigerator; mold spreading along floorboards and growing like ivy up the walls and across the ceiling. A mighty Mardi Gras Indian headdress swept away. A favorite blanket or dress left behind, now gone. So many photo albums, letters, birthday cards, and recipes lost in the water, forever. A loved one who was never supposed to die in the attic.

Everything was brown, then gray. Our lives had lost color, but we endured together.

For a time, we carried the pain as a part of ourselves. Every day the sorrow was there, unwilling to dissipate. Every conversation came back to the storm, every lonely walk made us wish our friends could come home. In time, our sorrow began to wane. Bit by bit, time smoothed the jagged edge of our memories. Families returned, communities regrouped. The grass turned green. Flowers bloomed. We could not do it alone. Faith-based, national, and college groups streamed in from across the country with supplies, working to gut houses and help us stand again. Neighbors helped one another. Together we took down drywall, stretched blue tarps across torn roofs, and began to rebuild. People reached out and came together in living rooms, churches, and community centers throughout the city. We cried and laughed, broke down and held others up, felt fear, felt guilt, felt frustration. We were battered, bruised, and scarred. But with grit, determination, and help, the people of this city rose out of the water, bearing the burden together that none of us could bear alone. Our resilience leads us down the path to resurrection.

When my father was mayor in the 1970s, he had 6,000 city employees. Nagin had as many as 6,300 in 2005 before Katrina; he was forced to lay off thousands after the flood. Sales tax revenues had crashed, leaving scant budget for salaries. Whatever Nagin's state in the hotel room that day, he had recovered to handle himself with the media and project a sense of control. I am not saying this cynically, or tongue in cheek. Many people I knew lost houses, cars, in many cases their savings in order to fund home or business rebuilding against what insurance covered; all of that took a heavy emotional and sometimes psychological toll. Countless people told me that prescriptions for antidepressant medications had skyrocketed in New Orleans. Those weeks and months were a nightmare I never want to experience again.

In the months after the storm, I turned the Department of Culture, Recreation and Tourism into an emergency recovery agency. With whole areas of New Orleans off the grid, and some neighborhoods in several feet of water for weeks after Katrina, I allocated space in the lieutenant governor's suite of rooms for the New Orleans City Council to meet privately and conduct public business as needed. My assistants threw in efforts to help people with flooded homes find temporary housing.

In the weeks it took to drain the city, Mayor Nagin and his team were overwhelmed. At the state level, it soon became clear that we were going to be investing in one of the toughest recoveries in American history. The extent of damage was mind-boggling enough; but the loss of political trust by the people was an open wound. Major foundations and nonprofits wanted to put fuel into the recovery, but City Hall under Nagin was ill equipped to send proposals with targeted needs, captured in clear prose, with well-developed budgets. The wasted opportunity made for long delays in rebuilding. I learned of one official in a major federal agency who had authority over a budget and who personally asked Nagin for a proposal, which he waved off, saying, "We're not able to handle that yet." Many of the foundations over time decided not to work directly with City Hall, and instead only with outside nonprofits and community groups. As lieutenant governor, I began engaging with them myself to preserve lines of cooperation and communication for when City Hall could handle it.

The Bush administration, Nagin, and Blanco were each plagued by distrust and dysfunction. The lack of coordination, agreement, and a unified strategy left Bush in a state of relative indifference, as he became obsessed with the Iraq war, while Nagin was counting on the White House to provide a great inflow of relief funds. As he waited, Nagin formed the Bring New Orleans Back Commission, relying heavily on Joe Canizaro, the downtown developer for whom my dad had once worked. Canizaro invited the Urban Land Institute, an organization of developers, architects, and planners, to draft a plan for rebuilding the city. Most people were still struggling to get back in the fall of 2005, but enough citizens showed up at the BNOBC hearings to rail against the new "urban footprint" that would let whole areas of flood-wracked New Orleans East, the Lower Ninth Ward, and the Broadmoor neighborhoods turn into unoccupied green spaces—buffers against future floods—while people in those areas were displaced. As protests rose, Nagin backed away from the ULI plan, saying that everyone had the right to return to where they wanted to live. He had no plan of his own.

Governor Blanco, meanwhile, launched the Louisiana Recovery Authority, chaired by Norman Francis and Walter Isaacson, the author and a New Orleans native son who had recently become the CEO at the Aspen Institute. As the LRA became a crossroads for foundation support, Blanco and the congressional delegation pressed for federal legislation that eventually produced the Road Home Program, to give grants to homeowners and businesses whose insurance policies left them short of rebuilding funds. The slow pace at which all of this took place was a case study in how *not* to respond after a national disaster. Many of us in government realized that the Stafford Act, the enabling legislation for FEMA and crisis response, was woefully outdated. FEMA needed a drastic overhaul; but that is not to shift blame from Louisiana.

Everyone working with Nagin knew he had been traumatized and was not providing the vision or leadership to spark a genuine recovery. His team was as erratic and disorganized as he was. In January 2006, he made his notorious "chocolate city" speech on Martin Luther King, Jr.'s birthday—saying that the Lord had spoken to him, and New Orleans would always be majority black. This is not the city that I knew—we were not a white city or a black city but a multicultural city. Like the Lost Cause arguments, this rang false to me. True, he was running for reelection; and African Americans had indeed borne a disproportionate share of the losses in the storm. The city needed massive help, but foundation grant officers were uneasy at the spectacle in City Hall. The city had failed to access federal pipelines. The "chocolate city" speech was a clear pitch to African Americans stuck in Atlanta, Baton Rouge, or

Houston, or sitting in FEMA trailers, angry at the Bush administration, angry at government period. Nagin, who had donated a thousand dollars to George W. Bush's 2000 campaign, and had won the mayoralty four years earlier with 70 percent of the white vote and only 30 percent of African Americans, now pinned his reelection on black voters, casting himself as the man they needed to keep hold of City Hall. The election turned into a racial litmus test.

Maybe I made a bad decision to enter that race and run against Nagin, and I have only myself to blame, but I hated to see the city I loved so broken. I had to find a way to make the African American base I had built see that a vote for me was not a vote against their self-interest. Had Nagin done a halfway decent job I would not have run for mayor; but I couldn't bear to sit passively at the sight of so much neglect, a fractured infrastructure, and flood-battered streets where six months after the storm dead cars layered in dirt still sat under the Claiborne Avenue overpass like carcasses waiting for a far-off burial. I felt that I could kick-start the recovery and begin to rebuild a city that had been torn apart.

It was, bar none, the worst campaign experience I ever had. People were tired and angry, the mood in the city fierce and intense. Although the recovery had hit a brick wall, Nagin was hungry to find redemption in the public eye. National civil rights groups organized voter transportation to get New Orleans evacuees in Atlanta, Houston, and other cities the opportunity to vote, either where they were staying under special arrangements or back in the city. I watched the support for Nagin build as we entered the runoff, and realized that the turn of events was beyond my capacity to control. Race trumps everything at a certain point. Many African Americans felt scorned by the Katrina debacle; they were afraid. He played on their fears of their city being taken from them—he would stand up to the Man and "take it back." Ironically, Nagin's top contributors were from wealthy, old-line white families who thought they could control the mayor. Voters were strewn all over the country. People voted from satellite locations in cities all over, literally. I campaigned in Atlanta and Houston, of all places. It was surreal.

In the end I got clipped and beaten. I was hurt, mostly because this was one of the few times I realized people viewed me as white. I was confused because these were the same African Americans my family and I had always fought so hard for. I had good public standing and could one day run for governor, but I felt sure I would never be mayor of New Orleans.

The recovery limped along without the major infusion of dollars needed to bring back streets, parks, and public spaces; the Road Home Program did provide grants for people to rebuild their houses and businesses, and to slowly gain a sense of normalcy to certain neighborhoods. But I dusted myself off and went back to work in Baton Rouge, and was not surprised when Mayor Nagin did not reach out to us for help.

My whole family went about doing what everyone else was—dealing with claims adjusters and contractors and the red tape necessary to get our homes rebuilt. After we got our moorings back, we created a family fund to rebuild the camp on Lake Pontchartrain. I thought of my grandpa Joe, patiently untangling those fishing lines we had jumbled together—steady of hand, determined to see his work through. It helps to have an example like that in your past.

I learned a lot during Katrina and its aftermath, about myself and my city. It's easier to reach for what was, rather than strive for something new. This is something true about people regardless of race or class. Katrina taught us that while we had come a long way in civil rights, the inequities that still existed were a result of the lingering shadow of Jim Crow. Race was an issue we'd have to confront directly if we were ever going to move our city and country forward.

CHAPTER 5

Rebuilding and Mourning in NOLA

Dreams really die hard. After the 2006 defeat I went back to the lieutenant governor's office. The post-Katrina racial divisions were like gaping wounds, and though Nagin struck me as in way over his head, the voters had spoken. I was determined to help the city as best I could.

In 2007 I ran for reelection as lieutenant governor. Despite a continuing shift of Louisiana voters to Republican candidates, I won in a landslide. GOP congressman Bobby Jindal, who had lost a close race to Blanco four years earlier, coasted to victory as governor.

I doubled down on strengthening tourism and the cultural economy, investing in historic preservation, and supporting service organizations and nonprofits doing such work. We developed a master plan to revitalize the New Orleans economy. I was comfortable as lieutenant governor, an office I had turbocharged. I liked being a catalyst for the tourism and hospitality industries, and in traveling the state learned more of the history and mix of rich cultures. I intended to run for governor in 2015. After all, I had twice been elected statewide without a runoff. My sister had just won a third senatorial term in a convincing fashion. My polling numbers were good statewide. I could help New Orleans from Baton Rouge, after all.

The recovery had flatlined under Nagin, which did not surprise me in light of his personality issues; but four and a half years after Katrina, the city's dismal condition kept gnawing at me. As the mayoral election in 2010 came into view, I wasn't impressed with the field lining up for the mayor's race, which included several wealthy businessmen. No disrespect to men and women of commerce, but government is not a business and the idea of "running government as a business," while a great line for TV spots, does not work as a political reality. Businesses function to earn profit; cities are governed to deliver public services, maintain infrastructure, and help businesses; they operate with revenue from taxation and grant support from state and federal government, as well as foundations. You can employ "best practices" to weed out rot or improve delivery of services; but you don't run a police department or any public works department to make a profit. My phone was ringing, with several state legislators urging me to run. Then I heard from James Carville.

James, Bill Clinton's great strategist, and his wife, Mary Matalin, who served in both Bush White Houses, had lucrative careers in political media when they left the Washington, D.C., area in 2008 and moved to New Orleans. They plunged into the life of the city, hosting events for civic causes—model public citizens. We became friends.

"You can not only win, but win in the primary," James told me. In New Orleans, all parties compete in one "open" primary, and if anyone wins over 50 percent, there is no need for further voting. Otherwise, the top two candidates go into a runoff, which becomes the general election.

As part of his professorship at Tulane University, Carville had conducted a survey on the mayor's race that sampled the views of a thousand people, a large number compared with normal surveys. The poll found voters frustrated with the sluggish recovery and racial divisions; more than two thirds thought the city was moving in the wrong direction. They wanted someone who could unite people and jump-start the rebuilding—not another outsider businessman like Ray Nagin, but a politician with governing experience. That suggested a case of buyers' remorse in voters who had rejected me the last time. In politics you never take support for granted—you have to earn the base every time, as I knew from my own recent outings. I was sure I could restore a city in severe disrepair, but would I get blindsided and lose again?

I made a late entry into the 2010 mayor's race, so late as to surprise close friends and family. I announced at an open event for Café Reconcile, the teaching restaurant founded by, among others, the late Father Harry Tompson, my mentor at Jesuit. Café Reconcile takes youth off the street, mostly out of school and in trouble, puts them through training in cooking, in front-of-the-house work, and in the kitchen—a full immersion for getting a job. The restaurant is on Oretha Castle Haley Boulevard, a street in the middle of town that had fallen into blight, named for a prominent civil rights leader of the 1960s. Resurrection and redemption come from unlikely places.

I won a majority in the primary going away, defeating African American business consultant Troy Henry and local businessman John Georges. They never gained traction in large part because they were perceived to be too much like Nagin. And now, years removed from the traumatic event itself, voters of all races were looking for steady leadership. More important to me than winning was *how* I won, gaining 66 percent of the overall vote and a majority of both African American and white votes. I lost only one out of the nearly four hundred precincts in New Orleans, and that one by just a single vote. I am still questioning our get-out-the-vote effort in that precinct. My election happened to come on the weekend when the New Orleans Saints won their first Super Bowl; the air was charged with optimism. For me it felt like a fresh start.

I began reaching out to hundreds of New Orleanians to serve on transition and planning task forces. I also contacted other mayors for advice: Michael Bloomberg of New York, Richard M. Daley of Chicago, Tom Menino of Boston, Michael Nutter of Philadelphia, Antonio Villaraigosa of Los Angeles, Anthony Williams of Washington, D.C., among others. Every city has its own unique concerns, but many issues overlap and I wanted to see how other mayors handled them.

Mayor Bloomberg, who became a mentor and a friend, told me two simple things I have never forgotten: "Hire a great scheduler because your time is your most valuable asset. And do all of the tough things first." His advice was superb, though I did not foresee how everything we faced would be tough— all the way to the end. Mike Bloomberg also introduced me to the deputy mayor system, which required hiring professionals with management skills to oversee the government. Having deputy mayors provides a boundary for the mayor's office, so that you're not at the beck and call of people who can be helped by high-level staff. This was a management system designed for better and faster results; it has worked.

Mayor Daley of Chicago advised on how to consolidate

various departments to make the bureaucracy work better across silos. Mayor Joseph P. Riley of Charleston, South Carolina, the dean of U.S. mayors, talked about how important city design, architecture, and planning was, which was particularly relevant to our recovery. Mayor Menino showed off his 311 and other technology systems, much of which we would later adopt, to help reform the way New Orleans government worked. Mayor Nutter took me into the daily battle for criminal justice reform.

My sister Mary, Louisiana's senior senator, was leading the recovery effort in Washington, D.C., and the whole Louisiana congressional delegation fought hard for our fair share of funding to rebuild schools, housing stock, hospitals, and more. Mary has never been given her due credit for the major work she did in helping the city recover. It took an army to get it done, but there would have been no resurgence without her strong leadership.

My term would open in the middle of another disaster, with nightly news footage of oil spewing out beneath the Gulf of Mexico at a broken well site. Several weeks before I took office, the Deepwater Horizon oil rig exploded offshore, killing eleven men. As oil gushed into the Gulf of Mexico unabated, the world again watched south Louisiana take another hit. The city's economy and well-being are utterly dependent on tourism, and everyone worried about the fishing industry as a major supplier of seafood to New Orleans restaurants. Would people still come here if they were afraid to eat our food after this? The economy took a hit.

I cannot overstate how broken our city government was at my inauguration in May 2010. The disarray was numbing; not only was the recovery stalled, but the city was at the brink of bankruptcy and NOPD was under federal investigation, not to mention four other major city agencies under federal consent judgments or management oversight due to poor performance and in some cases abuse.

I brought in consultants from the Public Strategies Group to conduct a forensic assessment of the city organization across the board. David Osborne told us that we had inherited "the least competent city government" and "the most corrupt—a really tough experience." He said plainly, "The city faces more challenges than we have ever seen in an American city."

The workforce had taken deep cuts, with many functions outsourced to contractors; payroll staff was down to about 4,000, well below the pre-Katrina 6,300. To save money, Mayor Nagin had moved City Hall to a four-day workweek. During the transition, I was told that the city had a $35 million deficit. When my team got into City Hall, we opened the books and after a thorough audit found that the budget deficit was actually $62 million, then $67 million, before finally settling on a $97-million gap. With only six months left in the year, and zero reserves, with no one-time Katrina funding or borrowing capacity, we had to close the city's budget gap— more than one fifth of the total general fund. We did so by reducing boards and commissions, reorganizing departments, and changing the delivery of core services. Even in the shrunken government, there was a lot of overlap and waste. We continued privatizing where we could. Instead of providing direct health care, we shut down our city clinics and transitioned the patients to primary-care health clinics with nonprofit operators, which were spread throughout the city. We were able to place nearly all of our employees with those private facilities. We also cut contracts large and small—the most controversial of which were three garbage collection contracts, two of which were the largest public contracts held by African American businesses in the state. It was painful and controversial because it was viewed racially in political circles, but nothing could be sacrosanct, and this was about fiscal waste, not race. I was also forced, reluctantly, to furlough city employees 10 percent of their time, a big hit for an already beleaguered group of public servants. This was a painful task, forcing good people to take personal losses.

The city's technology system was on the verge of collapse. Many critical systems—payroll, finance, revenue—all had single points of failure, which means that if one thing went wrong, the entire system stopped working. The city's Web server for e-mails kept going down. The most visible signs of systemic trouble were the many streets badly in need of repair. Nagin's recovery czar, Edward Blakely, had promised "cranes in the sky" within a year of his 2007 appointment. Not only had that building boom not materialized, the streets were still completely torn up from flooding.

Nagin had also outsourced much of the city's management; highly paid subcontractors were providing basic services like reception and administrative work. Why pay $70 an hour for a clerical staffer performing basic duties at City Hall? Meanwhile, under Nagin, some 655 capital projects had been designed, representing an estimated $1.5 billion in costs. There was only one problem. The city had $1.2 billion to pay for those projects from allotted FEMA funds. This shortfall meant that other important projects could not launch, because the last administration overspent on design without a real budget or bottom line. We had to go back to the drawing board.

We found waste everywhere—the Nagin administration

had paid more than fifty thousand dollars to store seventy thousand dollars' worth of unused furniture, still in boxes! The city had spent more than a hundred thousand dollars in grant funds on a recovery website that no one knew existed.

My theory was that by cutting with a scalpel and not a hatchet, as they often do in Washington, we could be positioned to better deliver services when the finances got better. It would also take constant reorganization, looking at what is and is not working to deliver services. At the same time, you have to invest in the things that will help you grow or produce long-term results, like retail stores that generate sales tax and auditors who improve collections. So much had ground to a halt after the storm.

From my role as lieutenant governor, I knew that Mayor Nagin and his team had failed to access money available in the federal pipeline. We started right away to rebuild the city's relationship with FEMA and began negotiating for funding streams. President Obama, FEMA administrator Craig Fugate, and HUD secretary and later OMB director Shaun Donovan were nothing short of remarkable. As we began the transition, I asked President Obama if he would lend us some people to help. This was a great benefit, as it allowed us in the transition to put in process what I call "horizontal and vertical integration," which simply means that the city works cooperatively with state and federal offices on a given dimension of rebuilding. Anything I wanted to do with federal money—whether it be through FEMA, HUD, or the Department of Agriculture—turned on having people from each agency in the room, from start to finish.

I asked the president to insist his FEMA directors at the regional level meet with me personally once a month; the initial sessions laid the foundation for more funding streams ahead. Beyond those top-level meetings, our teams met as often as necessary. The city of New Orleans owes a lasting debt of gratitude to President Obama for putting the White House behind our rebuilding agenda. FEMA promised to approve anything to which the law said we were entitled, provided we proved it was caused by the flood damage. On one hand, that was no problem: it had been documented quickly that the city flooded on such an epic scale because of man-made error by the Army Corps of Engineers in its design and management of the levee system. On the other hand, because many of the city's records flooded, it was often hard to prove exactly what was caused by prior neglect and what was caused by the levee failure. After some 750 meetings over eight years, we secured billions more in federal funding for schools, hospitals, parks, playgrounds, and critical infrastructure, particularly streets and drainage.

I was determined not just to build back the city that was, but to rebuild a stronger, more resilient city for the future. That meant improving all public structures, not just the Old World architecture of the French Quarter, the Greek Revival architecture of the Garden District and Uptown, or the quilt of shotgun and Victorian cottages that give many neighborhoods their character and that visitors think of as "real New Orleans." There's more reality beyond that. One example here will suffice.

The blandly named Youth Study Center was a prison for juvenile offenders, and had become a nightmare of scandals before the 2005 flood. The facility was beaten to death in Katrina. The juvenile court judge wanted to rebuild it as it had been. I said, "No. We're not building back something that the city did not get right the first time." I insisted that the detention facility—our new Juvenile Justice Center—have a wraparound service center so that the juvenile inmates would meet judges, prosecutors, and police, demonstrating to them that the adults who incarcerated them were not abandoning them, but offering their time to try to help them restructure their lives. We put in space to bring the public school system inside, behind the gates. An initial $7 million budget ballooned to $42 million through a series of negotiations with FEMA.

As we drew up the plan to rebuild the many schools trashed in the flood, we went back to FEMA over and over, basically saying, Look, you cannot give us just a little bit of money. We have to build smarter for the future, with building codes that afford resilience in the event of future flooding. This is an issue that many cities within coastal zones are facing in the age of sea rise. We also pointed out that the United States of America itself needs a coherent, forward-thinking national policy, and we were part of that process. In 2015, ten years after the storm, we secured $2.4 billion just to cover the most extensive street and water system repair in the city's history; unfortunately, the funding cannot always get to the ground soon enough. In the summer of 2017, we experienced major disruptions to our water, sewerage, and drainage systems' power plant, causing flooding and a boil water advisory. The long timeline of the Katrina funding and repairs had caught up with us. Nonetheless, I knew that this funding was something that would make a material difference in everyone's life every day.

Early on, I instituted the deputy mayor system, with lines of authority and a more manageable organizational chart that allowed us to rebuild the work force with a $1 billion total budget. I began recruiting professionals in fields of expertise that cities require to thrive. I also ensured that we had a diverse team, led by women and African Americans, young and experienced. Many of the brightest minds in urban planning were attracted to the idea of helping rebuild a major American city. We worked on integrating data and technology in our policy decision making. Our data analytics unit and performance management team put New Orleans on the map for government innovation. We also wanted to have a bottom-up and not a top-down government, so we created a team of neighborhood engagement officers who were assigned to work with neighborhood leaders and associations across the city, many of whom were leading the recovery in their neighborhoods in absence of the formal government.

My primary challenge was to rebuild public trust, to restore credibility, and to heal a city that was broken—economically, spiritually, racially. To clean up corruption and restore trust, I signed a series of executive orders to change the city's system of awarding contracts by creating a chief procurement officer and a new contracting process in which selection committees would meet in public. Contracts with the city of New Orleans would now be awarded based on proven expertise in the field, rather than on knowing the right people in government. We also opened doors of opportunity with the Disadvantaged Business Enterprises initiative, giving dozens more local and minority-owned companies a level playing field by requiring some subcontractor participation of small and minority firms on contracts. Many groups had pushed for these reforms for years. We instituted them in the first thirty days.

Heartbreakingly, many of the city's recreation facilities were in shambles—empty swimming pools, broken restrooms and lighting, flood-damaged ball fields. No one could even tell which playgrounds and camps were open; there was no list. NORD—the New Orleans Recreation Department—with its baseball parks and Carrollton Boosters games—was fundamental to my coming of age. I made an absolute priority of bringing that system back.

The condition of one playground and camp was particularly dispiriting. Raised in the Seventh Ward neighborhood of Tremé (now famous from the HBO television series), Jerome Smith was a legendary civil rights activist and Freedom Rider in the 1960s in Mississippi. When he moved back to the Tremé neighborhood, he founded the Tambourine and Fan Club, an education and recreation program for youngsters with a summer camp at a place called Hunter's Field. A commanding role model with a gentle touch, Jerome Smith created a safe haven for kids who needed one—a place to laugh and learn, a respite from the unforgiving streets. Jerome Smith was a frontline leader in the battle for the soul of our city. Addicts and pushers learned to avoid Hunter's Field.

After Katrina, Mr. Smith had bad dealings with the Nagin people and some members of the City Council; the bureaucracy botched his request for basic supplies for the summer camp—no board games, no crayons, no Hula-Hoops. He still didn't close his doors or turn kids away. The heat index exceeded 100 degrees many days, and Mr. Smith's building did not have air-conditioning. So he brought in fans and kept the doors open; the kids kept coming. There was a raggedy bus to take the kids to a rundown old pool. For many kids, that was the only ride they'd take to someplace else, that pool their only escape from hot summer streets. The camp gave them a choice—and more than that, it gave them hope. Despite the city's many challenges, we committed early on to rebuilding

NORD by doubling the funds even as we worked through hard deficits. We made sure Tambourine and Fan received the supplies and funding it needed. We also rebuilt the Tremé Center, which now stands as a beacon of hope and a place of safe-haven in this historic neighborhood.

The good news I seized on, five years after Katrina, was that people kept coming back. Three areas hardest hit in the flood—New Orleans East, Gentilly, and the Ninth Ward—now had about eighty thousand residents. The bad news was that they faced a thirty-minute drive to an emergency room. It took several years for us to build a $140 million, eighty-bed hospital in New Orleans East as a neighborhood anchor.

With great foundation support, we started building infrastructure aimed at attracting private-sector investment and jobs. Resilient New Orleans, the country's first comprehensive resilience strategy, included innovative ways for how we can better live with water, such as investing in green infrastructure like rain gardens and bioswales. It covered actions to combat climate change, including increasing the use of cleaner modes of transportation and mobility, such as bicycles. But the strategy also included connecting vulnerable populations with the workforce skills needed to compete for the jobs created by our investments. We began tackling issues of violence reduction and racial equity, and connecting those who need work with the skills needed to service the private sector.

By 2015, ten years after the storm, New Orleans had the reputation as a cutting-edge leader in how to rebuild stronger and smarter. The city was growing. We'd turned around the city finances. We had been a declining city before the storm, we now had a future that was brighter.

In the final months of my second term, the New Orleans

economy has thrived, adding more than twenty thousand new jobs since 2010. We had recruited GE Capital Technology Center to the city with former governor Bobby Jindal, adding six hundred high-paying tech jobs, along with game developers and software creators. That, and aggressive digital and software development tax credits, provided groundwork for the single largest economic development announcement in New Orleans history, in November 2017, when DXC Technology, a Fortune 150 company, announced the arrival of a digital transformation center with two thousand jobs. A key factor was the infrastructure of colleges in the area with science and technology courses germane to DXC's hiring stream.

Today, spending from tourism has surpassed pre-Katrina highs. The *Wall Street Journal*'s MarketWatch named New Orleans one of the "most improved cities for business." New retail is booming, and in many areas surpassing pre-Katrina levels. The city has become a hub of entrepreneurship activity, outpacing the national per capita average by 56 percent. We have seen more than $8 billion in private development since May 2010. As a result of growth and confidence in the market, property values are up 50 percent. We've begun construction on a new, nearly $1 billion airport terminal, which will add major international flights and improve global business opportunities in the region.

Cities hold together by the quality of their people. New Orleanians by their nature are a hopeful, resilient people. In the last twelve years, we have been through hell and high water in this city, not just with Katrina, but Hurricanes Rita, Ike, Gustav, Isaac, the BP oil spill, and the national recession. But as the Mardi Gras Indian chant goes, "We won't bow down." After everything that we've been through, a poll of New

Orleans residents on the tenth anniversary of Katrina done by the Kaiser Family Foundation with NPR found that a whopping 78 percent of residents are optimistic about the city's future. New Orleans rebounded after 80 percent of the city was underwater in 2005, much of it for several weeks, to become one of the fastest-growing major cities in America, with thousands of new jobs, new industries, rapidly improving schools, rising property values, and a new, stronger flood protection system that will reduce the risk from hurricanes.

This is not to say New Orleans does not have problems. We still rank too high on the income inequality list. The local criminal justice system still disproportionately impacts African Americans. Unemployment among African Americans has been three times that of whites. Gentrification and the lack of affordable housing is a real issue in far too many of our neighborhoods. And African Americans are more likely to live in poverty and to attend poor schools than whites.

Let's be honest: before Katrina, the public school system was a disgrace. White flight from integration sparked decades of disinterest, decline, and disinvestment. By and large they were schools where the poorest and, frankly, mostly black students were left to try to scrape out an education. Corruption and gross mismanagement by the local school board only made it worse.

Katrina destroyed 110 of 127 schools, and when we went to rebuild, we felt there was almost nothing in them worth saving. The charter school movement that arose after Hurricane Katrina has brought a great improvement for youngsters. With $1.8 billion in federal funds invested to rebuild, renovate, or refurbish nearly every school in the city, we have outstanding learning spaces to help our kids thrive and realize their huge God-given potential. People argue about whether the charter school movement is the right way to approach education reform. Many vested schoolteachers lost their jobs and benefits after the legislature mandated a takeover of the school system following the 2005 disaster. A class action suit by 7,500 public-school teachers, mostly African American and women, won a large judgment from the state, only to be overturned by the State Supreme Court. Because of the way it was resolved, there remains some racial tension about this adult issue.

Nevertheless, the charter schools, which supplanted most of the old Orleans Parish system, have been an unparalleled success. Students are graduating at higher rates; the dropout rates are lower. The number of failing schools has dwindled to 7 percent from a pre-Katrina peak of nearly 60 percent. Before Katrina, the achievement gap between African American children in the city—the kids people said couldn't learn—and white youngsters in schools in the suburbs and the rural areas was more than 25 points. Now that gap has been nearly closed.

Today, nearly every student attends a public charter school and families who used to have only one choice for their kids can now apply to almost every school in the city. In New Orleans, geography no longer defines a kid's destiny; we've raised the bar across the board, insisting that schools serve every child, because in New Orleans we know that every child can learn and every child has the right to a great education.

Early in my life, Dr. Norman Francis drilled into me how important an education was to helping kids, particularly young African American kids, succeed in communities like New Orleans. Having a shot at an excellent education, despite your race or socioeconomic status, is the real way to level a playing field that is still unbalanced by the legacy of Jim Crow.

Before Katrina, the high school graduation rate hovered

around 50 percent. Now, almost three quarters of our kids are graduating on time, with more kids enrolling in college than ever before. One of these New Orleans high school graduates is a young man named Jairron Isaac. A few years ago, he wasn't going to pass the tenth grade, let alone go to college. His mom and dad sold drugs; both went to prison. As you can imagine, he struggled; but he enrolled in a charter school with a special focus on college. This made the pivotal difference. As Jairron said: "In life you have two choices, to be defeated or to conquer. I choose to conquer." In 2010, Jairron enrolled at Morehouse College, one example of the very real impacts the new system of schools is having. That's not to say we are close to perfect. Poverty is a huge deterrent to many children, but we are forging pathways for those who learn to find a new plateau.

Along with schools, health care is crucial. A dozen years ago, if a kid without a regular doctor or insurance had an earache, his mom faced a thirteen-hour wait time at the Charity Hospital emergency room just to get it checked out. In the last eight years we established a network of neighborhood health clinics with federal support. Dr. Karen DeSalvo, the New Orleans health commissioner, guided this process as a precursor to the Affordable Care Act, and later became President Obama's acting assistant secretary of Health and Human Services. The St. Thomas Community Health Center, as an example, handles everything from chronic disease management to pediatrics, with a special focus on women's health, conducting thousands of mammograms every year. Neighborhood health centers like St. Thomas serve 59,000 patients across the city every year, reducing the overload, and expense, at hospital emergency rooms. Two major hospitals are going up in the city, a Veterans Administration hospital and, adjacent to it, the University Medical Center, part of the LSU system.

The city's pre-Katrina "big four" public housing projects were decaying, crime-ridden horrors that hardly gave the poor what they needed or what they deserved. These complexes were demolished in the Nagin administration. With HUD support we've invested more than $1 billion in public housing—creating over 14,000 affordable rental units for low-income families. We've emphasized building homes close to schools, health care, and transit. We can see the difference it's made already at the former St. Bernard Development, now known as Columbia Parc. The St. Bernard was one of the old public housing developments first built by the Roosevelt Administration during the Depression. It had crumbled over the years. By the time Katrina hit, 25 percent of the 1,300 units were empty and the area was known for its violence. And then the levees broke, and as the sun rose the day after the storm passed, the St. Bernard Development was ten feet under water. We resolved to build back the St. Bernard not as it once was, but as it ideally should have been. Now, Columbia Parc is a mixed-income public-housing neighborhood that embraces public-private partnerships. The master plan for the neighborhood includes newly built schools, an early-childhood learning center, a recreation facility, a library, playgrounds, retail stores, and green space. And the crime rate has plunged.

With such historic poverty, New Orleans still has many disparities, some of them glaring. But as we enter 2018, the Tricentennial of our founding, New Orleans is a far better city than it has been in my lifetime, and a remarkable American comeback story. Rebuilding the city has been the most rewarding experience of my career in public life, second only to the happiness of raising a family with Cheryl. The best impulses of America show themselves when people work hard, dream of something better, and come together to make it happen. At times in the last eight years I was jarred by the scope of neglect and damage; my head and my heart told me that nothing is broken here or in America that cannot be repaired, no problem cannot be solved. The road is long; it takes sacrifice and is often painful. But we can get there, we can rebuild the city that so many of us dreamed New Orleans could be, had we gotten it right the first time. To do that, we had to be honest about our past and look to the future.

And, as every parent knows, you can only be as happy as your saddest child.

The shadow story of my city's stirring comeback is the price we pay in the horrific loss of human life through gun violence, most of which erupts in the poorest parts of town. In America, we have become anesthetized to the pace of such homicides, one more numbing thirty seconds on the nightly news, much less the mass shootings that at times seem like some curse that our religious leaders cannot explain. Any politician venturing into this terrain risks being derided as a soft liberal, a knee-jerk on gun control, or some dewy-eyed idealist, pining for a world where people behave well and all children are safe. Fine. I absolutely want a city, and a country, where children are safe. Yet as the mayor of every large municipality knows, the first law of governing is pragmatism, forging a balance between what we must do to foster growth and accepting the limits of what we cannot do. The question for me is how we change those limits.

My cell phone hums all hours of the day. Michael Harrison, the chief of police, sends me a text each time someone is killed. I try to visit the crime scenes and comfort the families who have lost their young. It is the most excruciating task I have as mayor.

The names follow me.

Ricky Summers. Briana Allen. Shawanna Pierce. Jeremy Galmon. Keira Holmes. Marcus McNeil. Daryle Holloway.

All were human beings who were shot and killed on the streets of New Orleans in my time as mayor, and these are only a handful of the hundreds who died while I was in office. Some names haunt me, track me, sneak in and out of my dreams. Others, from further back in the past, stay with me for their own reasons. James Darby. Michael Norfleet. Joseph Norfleet. Senseless deaths, senseless quarrels, bullets that halted lives that deserved America's promise.

If it is true that one person can change the world, it must be true that the absence of so many must change it as well.

In my eight years as mayor, the hardest day was May 29, 2012, when five-year-old Briana Allen died. It was her cousin Ka'Nard's tenth birthday, and they were celebrating on their grandmother's front porch. Balloons. Streamers. Music.

I remember my childhood birthday parties. One year, I got a pair of cowboy boots, another one brought a pair of big old boxing gloves. Standard cake and ice cream. Nothing was standard about the party where Briana was shot through her tiny midsection by an AK-47 bullet. She fell into the arms of her father, Burnell, who held her as she died.

Burnell was the intended target, a lifetime member of the notorious Allen family gang. During the party, two guys from the 3NG gang rounded the corner and saw Burnell on the porch. They didn't care that he was standing in the middle of small children, old folks, aunts, uncles, and friends. They let it rip. One bullet found Briana's gut—game over. Another bullet grazed her cousin Ka'Nard on the neck. A third bullet traveled three hundred yards down the street, crashed through a windshield, and exploded in Shawanna "Nonni" Pierce's head. Pierce, a young single mother of three young boys, Kelby, Kolby, and Khody, had just turned the corner on her way to return a rental car after leaving a son's graduation party. Just like that—gone.

The sun baked the shocked crowd at the party. Briana's grandmother screamed in agony. The police tape stretched for blocks, flapping in the summer wind. Twenty-three rounds fired, five people hit, two dead. In some neighborhoods, this is another day on the streets of America. As Briana's father held her tiny head in his hands, the blood pooled on the porch beneath birthday balloons, life seeping out of her, another loss, another wound in the city. Even as people gasped and mourned, the killings found other streets and fresh victims.

I had already made stopping the homicides a priority of my administration. But on that day, a counteroffensive to gun violence became my number-one consuming focus. I have often said that I didn't choose this. The crisis grabbed me. And today, it remains my morning coffee and my nighttime prayer. I pray that we can turn our culture from one of death and violence into one of peace and life.

I have kept a photo of little Bri-Bri, as they called her, in my office since that time. Her smiling face stares at me as a reminder of why this work is important. It is critical to my city's and our country's future.

What happens to the lives left behind?

Briana's father was soon arrested for another murder. He is now serving life behind bars. Briana's uncle would be dead within the year, ambushed by two men with assault rifles. The true epilogue to this terrible story is actually prologue for the future of New Orleans. It is about little Ka'Nard Allen. It was his birthday party that was interrupted by gunfire. He was hit in the neck that day. But for the grace of God, Ka'Nard survived, although he could not escape the violence all around him. Five months later, Ka'Nard's father was fatally stabbed by his stepmother. And then, nearly a year to the day of his cousin Briana's death, Ka'Nard was again caught in the crossfire, this time shot in the cheek along with eighteen others at a Mother's Day parade. Twice this boy came within inches of getting his head blown off. We expect little kids like Ka'Nard to soldier on, stand on their own two feet. Is that the best we can do? Could you, or I, bounce back, move on? His other scars run deep, but are not yet visible to us.

We have seen this all before. Why is the political will missing to respond with a countermeasure, *a policy*, as a civilized people should?

Let me take you back to another Mother's Day, this time 1994. Families were picnicking at A. L. Davis Park in Central City. Nine-year-old James Darby was playing a pickup football game. A little girl got elbowed in the face during a fracas; she went home in tears. Her father had left the family. Her older brother, Joseph Norfleet, nineteen, the man of the house, was that day drunk and high. He saw his sister's black eye and flew into a rage. Egged on by an older stepbrother, he grabbed a shotgun and jumped in a car. It was a short trip back to A. L. Davis Park. Joseph stuck his shotgun out the window and shot into the crowd, aiming for someone else in the Darby family but instead hitting James in the head, killing him instantly. Nine years old. Just a few weeks earlier, James Darby had written President Clinton:

Dear Mr. Clinton,

I want you to stop the killing in the city. People is dead and I think that somebody might kill me. So would you please stop the people from deading. I'm asking you nicely to stop it. I know you can do it. Do it. I now you could.

Your friend,
James.

We use that overused word *tragic* to describe terrible events, and in this case for tragedy at both ends of the gun. The pain and agony of losing not one child, but two. James died and was buried in cold ground. And Joseph, nineteen, lit up and showing a child's bullying bravado in what he did, went to the Louisiana State Penitentiary at Angola for the rest of his life. Several years ago I went to see him at Angola. It was surreal. He spoke of the day he now regrets. He spoke of having been shot twice in his life on the rough streets of New Orleans before that day. We are left to wonder what might have been. As the years pass, we talk about violence just as "part of the culture." Each murder becomes one small part of some impossibly large whole.

I am haunted by the lives we could not save. The river of federal funds that allowed me to rebuild this city provided no levee system against the tides of violence sprung from the porous gun laws of this country. I had no power to stop the flow of guns; the criminal justice system can only arrest and incarcerate the worst offenders. In the face of futile gun laws, I decided to raise awareness and set an alternative path. We have made a significant dent, but it is only that, a dent. We have so much more work to do. I firmly believe that this is a solvable problem if we treat gun violence as both a public safety issue *and* a public health crisis. We vaccinate people to thwart disease. Against gun violence, society is passive.

A politician learns from youngsters trapped on the front lines of this carnage how desperately they want to avoid drug gangs and *change their circumstances.* Ricky Summers, sixteen, was surrounded by violence in his Central City neighborhood. Ricky was determined to get out and be different. He was one of the original "KIPPsters" enrolled in the first class at Knowledge Is Power Program in Central City, part of the charter school effort. With ambitions for college, Ricky was struggling to become a man without the guiding hand of a father. His eighth-grade English class had been studying Langston Hughes's poem, "Harlem." "What happens to a dream deferred? Does it dry up like a raisin in the sun? . . . *Or does it explode?*"

Ricky was in his school uniform when they found him behind a blighted house, shot in the back. Ricky's dream was violently denied, his rich potential snuffed out like too many before him. What must we do to save young men like Ricky Summers?

Not too far from Briana Allen's photo are stacks of red binders in my office. They hold the stories of murder victims in my city—more than one thousand of them since I took office in 2010. Emotions overflow at funeral services. Another prayer vigil, a moment of silence, an endless cycle, primarily young African American men killing each other.

In 2011, five John McDonogh High School students were killed before they had a chance to make their mark on the world. It is a sad, horrifying truth that in 2011, a John McDonogh High student was more likely to be killed on New Orleans streets than a soldier fighting in Afghanistan. Let that sink in.

Statistics confirm that 80 percent of the victims know one another. Most of the "beefs" or disputes are so petty as to leave us numb over the waste of human life. Day after day young men kill someone they know, and not just in New Orleans. They are not faceless, nameless thugs who die out of sight and mind; they are flesh and blood. They matter. Their deaths are not God's will. Often, as I have tried to focus attention on this issue, many people, not just whites, turn away. *Not my problem . . . Just thugs killing thugs . . . They get what they deserve . . . It's not my fault.*

One of the biggest sticks that was used against me in taking down monuments was that I should be focused on murder, not monuments. Not one of those people helped me in fighting murder or helping young, black men in my time at City Hall. And my record on murder reduction is unlike any other administration. But the opponents to taking down the monuments used any excuse they possibly could.

The great civil rights activist and congressman John Lewis refused to stand aside, asking, "If not us, then who? If not now, then when?"

Our battlefield is on the street and in the heart. The mass shootings in churches, schools, movie theaters, and malls are the opposite face of the same coin: too many guns, too little preventive intervention. This is a mental health issue, a security issue, and the greatest moral issue in America today. Where are the voices of our religious leaders, calling down the failure of legislators and government to face this blight? If this is not a pro-life issue, what on God's earth is it?

Since at least the early 1970s, major urban centers have experienced gunfire like warfare. Every year, nearly fifteen thousand people are murdered on American soil—about forty people lost every twenty-four hours. In Las Vegas, before the horrific massacre from the hotel window of people attending a country-music concert, a life went down to gun violence on average once a day. That bears repeating: In most major cities, someone dies each day from a gunshot. The weapon of choice, most often a handgun; the victims and perpetrators disproportionately young African American men.

As former Philadelphia mayor Michael Nutter has so forcefully said, if a foreign enemy killed fifteen thousand American citizens, there would be hell to pay. If the Ku Klux Klan murdered thousands of young black men, this nation would be in an uproar. But for some reason we are hardened to domestic gun deaths and remain eerily silent. Maybe it is in slow motion—we refuse to hear it or see it because we place too little value on the lives of young, black men.

This humanitarian crisis is not in some far-off nation, but here on our streets, in our neighborhoods, in our homes. America cannot be strong abroad if we are under attack at home. Morally, economically, and for the good of this nation's strength and security, we must change this hideous situation. It is wrong for police officers to patrol streets in crime-ridden areas at a disadvantage in weapons. As president of the United

States Conference of Mayors, I worked with my colleagues in proposing policies to increase mental health facilities, reduce prison terms for nonviolent offenders, and broaden programs to reach at-risk youth. We want to limit the guns and strengthen the rules about who can buy them and what they can buy. We must get Congress to address the cadaver in the living room, as Republican and Democratic mayors, police chiefs, and law enforcement officials have done.

From 1980 to 2012, a total of 626,000 people, a disproportionate number of them African American men, were murdered in America. That's more citizens lost to murder in thirty-two years than all of our servicemen killed during World War I, World War II, Korea, Vietnam, the Persian Gulf War, and the wars in Iraq and Afghanistan *combined*. I refuse to accept that America is so callous about human life. This must stop.

The response in Congress has been tepid because of the racial dynamics: most of the victims are young blacks, not part of the Republican base, not worth the risk of offending the powerful National Rifle Association. People are scared to speak up. Or perhaps, as a nation, we have bought into an evil notion—that the lives of these mostly young African American men killed every day have less value and thus don't deserve our urgent attention.

Instead of grappling with this problem, we desperately look for quick fixes and want to "get tough"—more prisons, more guards, more guns. But history tells us that that will just make things worse. We can't imprison our way out of this problem. America has more people incarcerated than more than a dozen other countries combined. And many nations with fewer people in prison have less crime and lower murder rates. Since the early 1980s, the number of incarcerated people in the United

States has increased more than fourfold, going from less than a half million to about 2.2 million people today. That increase is more than double the rate of inflation over the same period. In Louisiana alone, since 1990, the population in prison has more than doubled, from about 19,000 to about 40,000 today. That leaves about 1 in 86 adults in our state incarcerated, with nearly half serving sentences for nonviolent, mostly drug-related offenses. America spends about $70 billion every year on corrections, roughly on par with the budget for the entire Department of Education. Indeed, on average, public schools spend about $12,000–$13,000 per pupil per year. To incarcerate one person for one year costs about $30,000, depending on the state. In two decades, Louisiana went from spending about $275 million on incarceration to $750 million today. Remember Joseph Norfleet? The state will spend several million dollars keeping him behind bars for life. And Louisiana's violent crime rate is higher now than it was in 1977.

I have seen it up close, standing over the body of a young African American boy, gunned down like a dog, lying on the street, eyes open, tongue protruding, lifeless. You stare and think this should not be.

You look paralyzed at the police officer in the operating room of our trauma unit, a gunshot to the head. You think this should never be. I have seen more than I want to see. But once you've seen something, you can't unsee it.

I attend as many of the funerals as I can. The city owes the families some presence, a sign that we grieve with them, knowing things aren't right. It is hard beyond words to put yourself close to a family shattered by violent loss. It is a duty I will not miss when I'm not mayor. But in fulfilling this responsibility, I have come to see that whether mother or father, son or daughter, grief is not filtered by whether the deceased was a police officer, an innocent child, or a young man with a rap sheet, "in the life." When you are standing at the casket and hear the sobs and feel the heartache around you, the distant cries of Black Lives Matter and Blue Lives Matter fade as you realize that we are all losers in this culture of violence. *This is a problem that can be fixed.* It requires a national, holistic policy in public health—not unlike our efforts to contain Ebola or our newfound recognition that the opioid epidemic needs a sweeping commitment to mental health and substance abuse treatment.

Treating the cause and not just the symptom is important. It was not done in the 1980s and '90s when we locked up mostly African American crack cocaine users and threw away the key. We had a "war on drugs." "They" were criminals and had to be dealt with by the justice system, political leaders argued. But yet today, with a mostly white face on the opioid crisis in the Rust Belt and the northeast, we're talking in much more holistic, public health terms. There is empathy and compassion for those with addiction. Policymakers today talk about destigmatizing drug addiction. Police are being trained to administer Narcan, a drug that saves the lives of those overdosing. These are good changes, but I worry about the lingering effects of the old mentality. Black men and women are still in prison for drug possession charges decades ago, and so the cycle continues.

And so you might ask, with so much urban warfare in the poorest streets, how have we responded as a nation? Even little kids can tell you, "Out here it is kill or be killed"—that cold, that simple. Yet for too many Americans, this reality may as well be on another planet. Murder and violence are the poisonous fruit grown from the soil of injustice, racism, and inequality—fertilized by guns, drugs, alcohol, and disinte-grated families. Hope fades, hate grows, people feel they have nothing to lose. To those who say it has always been this way, I answer: We made this problem by neglect; we can be proac-tive and fix it.

All of this happens in the shadows of statues whose message has always been, as Terence Blanchard said: African Americans are less than.

Every murder leaves a wake of destruction, the collateral damage of gunshots. An innocent child loses a father; a mother's heart is broken; a family is sent reeling into an abyss. But the endings don't have to be entirely bleak. Consider Leonard Galmon. Leonard's father was killed on the streets of New Orleans when he was four; his seventeen-year-old mother was alone. As Leonard moved through school, he found a path in the Recovery School District that led him to Cohen College Prep, a charter school. With the help of his teachers, Leonard applied to colleges and universities. He was accepted to Yale University with a full scholarship. Leonard's story made the front page of the press, and more articles and editorials fol-lowed. He was honored by the City Council and the State Legislature. Congratulations and donations flooded in from across the city; he showed the determination to find a way. He had good help, which is what many more young African American men on the bitter edge need in order to turn them-selves around; they, too, can do great things with the right support and guidance.

Those of us who had easy paths to education should realize how steep the odds are for first-generation college students;

only one in ten who start college actually graduate. With hats off to Leonard Galmon, I look forward to the day when it will *not* be front-page news when a young African American from New Orleans is accepted by Yale, because so many others followed in Leonard's path.

Imagine with me two children representing the hundreds of kids living on opposite sides of oak-lined St. Charles Avenue, the famous street with the streetcar tracks. They live a few blocks away from each other, but a world apart in every other sense. In Central City, a boy named James, fourteen, goes to public school; he lives on Seventh Street with his mom and two younger brothers, a few blocks downriver from St. Charles. A one-bedroom apartment in a long, thin, rundown building. Every morning, James's mom catches the 5:30 bus to a downtown hotel. She won't get back from her second job as a security guard until nine that night. James gets home from school. Not much is going on in the afternoon. As the sun sets, James is restless, hangs with friends at his corner. His mom tries her best, but the drugs, easy money, and guns are everywhere, and most of the time no one's at home to help him resist the lure of the street. One day, James's mom finds a pistol under his bed. Imagine young James, in tears, telling her the same thing I have heard from kids just as young: "It's for *protection*." Again, I hear: "Mayor, out here it's either kill or be killed."

Meanwhile, four blocks on the upriver side of St. Charles, at a home in the Garden District, another fourteen-year-old, Mike, goes to private school. The family lives in a large four-bedroom house. Mom is a lawyer, Dad's in finance. They're good people, working long hours downtown, but the nanny is home for Mike when school lets out, unless he's at practice for the tennis, football, or basketball teams, or stays for Chess

Club or Quiz Bowl practice. Every night, the family eats dinner; Mom or Dad makes sure he does homework. Mike in the Garden District hopes to follow in Dad's footsteps. James in Central City: his dad's in Angola prison.

On Mardi Gras, the two boys head to St. Charles Avenue, drawn by the exotic splendor of the Zulu King, the beauty of the Rex parade, the backbeat of the St. Augustine Purple Knights Marching 100, the bounce of Al Johnson's voice singing "Carnival Time" in a truck parade.

James watches from the lake side of St. Charles, Mike from the river side. For a brief moment, they occupy the same world, hearts beating to the same rhythm, catching beads and dancing in the same street. In between floats, as kids play in the street, perhaps they meet or reach for the same pair of beads, joined in the synthesis of time, geography, culture, race, and music, all shared, touching the same reality, things they both want, perfect symmetry for one moment in time.

But when the parade ends, they go back to their lives on different sides of St. Charles Avenue, to different worlds.

In James's Central City, the average household income is less than $36,000. In Mike's world, in the Garden District, the average household income exceeds $128,000. In Central City, 69 percent of households are run by a single parent, mostly a mother. In the Garden District, only 3 percent are single parent households. In Central City, people are twice as likely to rent rather than own, five times as likely not to have a vehicle. To make ends meet, the mom earning minimum wage must work day and night, typically two jobs; latchkey kids wait hours for Mom to come home.

Since 2010, Central City has seen more than three hundred shootings. Walk a few blocks away, it is a different world; there were only two shooting victims in the Garden District over the last seven years. Think again about fourteen-year-olds, James and Mike, each walking home that Mardi Gras night. For James, as on many nights in Central City, NOPD searched the area after a shooting. Witnesses say it was a young black man in a hoodie. Cops, already on edge, see James with his hood up and pull toward him fast and close. James jerks his hand out of his pocket. He is holding a black cell phone. Will the police know that? Sometimes this is how tragedies happen, and for young men like James, the margin of error between life and death is razor thin. If we replace James with Mike from the Garden District, the difference in that margin of error would likely allow Mike to live.

These same two neighborhoods produced Joseph Norfleet and Peyton Manning. They're about the same age and may have played on the same football team at the nearby A. L. Davis playground some thirty years ago. Imagine them meeting in some football scrimmage and then going their separate ways. One on a pipeline to prison, the other to NFL prosperity.

Some people are cynical and say we cannot change. I believe we can. The great part of being American is that we believe in endless horizons, that for every problem there is a solution, that no breach or divide cannot be repaired. I have hope because of young people like Leonard Galmon. Out of despair, hope rises. Leonard went to Yale because hope was his compass.

In 2012 we launched a program called NOLA for Life with the stated agenda of reducing homicide and giving youngsters on the margins activity and structure as our budget allowed.

We asked police officers, mothers of murder victims, crimi-nologists, focus groups with young men "in the life," How can we reduce this problem? Can we find a strategy worth applying on a greater level? Each group told us essentially the same things: solutions for prevention have to be visible on the streets. You have to change a lot in a given culture to reduce murders when killing is so widespread. More jobs, good schools, healthy neigh-borhoods, stronger families, a better police department—all play a pivotal role; we also learned that murders happen in small groups of young African American men who hang out together.

The same profile emerges time and again. Roughly one in three murders happens in the same four neighborhoods, and 80 percent of the victims are young black males. Many are high school dropouts and unemployed. Eighty percent had an arrest record; more than half of them are under twenty-nine, and close to 80 percent of the murderers knew their victims. After talking to young men who fit the profile, we learned that they want to get out of the life. We go to those young men doing violence and we literally sit them down and say, "We value you, we love you. Put down the gun and we can help you. If you don't, we will take action to protect the city."

Sometimes the opportunity to make a change helps us get someone on the right track. I think about one young man who dealt drugs, carried a gun, ran with a crew. When he got in-volved with NOLA for Life, he came with two of his partners. Before the end of the year, one of them would be arrested for murder and the other would be shot dead. But he chose a new way. With our help, he got a job, worked hard, and has been promoted. He got off the streets and into a local community college. He is building a life for himself and his young children.

The other piece to this murder-prevention strategy is a

local, state, and federal Multi-Agency Gang Unit. It has targeted 14 violent groups, gotten 150 individuals indicted, and by using RICO racketeering statutes, put dozens of gang members behind bars. The message we send to those terrorizing our neighborhoods is: You have a choice. Stop the shooting, put down your gun, and we will help you get on the right path— or we are coming for you. We don't have all the answers, but we're focused on supporting young men who turn away from the violence. With Michael Nutter and several philanthropic foundations we started Cities United, which brings together mayors from across the country to address the violence among African American men.

CeaseFire New Orleans seeks to stop the cycle of violence by mediating conflicts; hundreds of youth from the toughest New Orleans neighborhoods come out for Midnight Basketball to play, learn from role models, and get connected to a chance for jobs and job training. We are working hard to help ex-offenders get their life back on track, with programs like Café Reconcile. This piece is really important to break the cycle. A third of the million prisoners released each year will go back to jail within three years.

Now, we can wait until they commit another crime, or we can anticipate their needs and meet them partway with job training, counseling, and employment offices. We've got to shut this revolving door. It is outrageous that one in fourteen black men is behind bars, and one in seven is either in prison, on parole, or on probation. To fight violent crime and murder we can't ignore the social dysfunction that causes it.

New Orleans has become a laboratory for social change with promising results. We launched an aggressive post-incarceration reentry strategy—a program that reaches out within seventy-two hours of release from prison and connects the ex-inmates with a workforce reentry program of services and jobs. Murder is at a historic quarter-century low. That is not easy for people to believe when the nightly news reports so much killing. I am not blaming the news media for doing their job. We still have too many murders, but we keep searching for the truth about city streets and how to stop the worst of it. We have a long way to go, but how far we have come.

I want historians who look back on this time to write about the people who met their terrible crisis of human rights *in America* and did what was just and decent to make the fundamental changes to uphold life in the poorest streets. The lives of children depend on it. Jefferson's words "All men are created equal" require a constant evaluation of ourselves.

Until *every life* matters, including black lives, we won't be able to plant seeds of hope in beleaguered neighborhoods and fulfill America's lofty promises. I believe that we are bound together as one people, indivisible, with one shared destiny. We cannot allow young black men to feel forsaken. We must go forward together or not at all. We must press on, share the agenda that the culture of homicides is evil and unacceptable, and resolve ourselves to changing it, however long it may take or incremental it may be. But to do so requires us to value every life. The monuments hover and tell a different story. The shadow these symbols cast is oppressive. It is in this broad context that people must now understand that the monuments and the reasons they were erected were intended not to affirm life but to deny life. And in that sense, the monuments in a way are murder.

CHAPTER 6

The Shadow of Robert E. Lee

A reelection campaign reflects what voters think of the job you have done in the preceding years. In 2014, I won a second term, prevailing handily over two opponents, earning 64 percent in the primary. We had scores of construction projects under way, extensive repair of streets and subsurface piping, and though crime was on many minds, not least my own, we were making headway in giving black boys from broken streets a path to hope with the resources available. Homicide rates were trending down significantly, though one killing is too many, as my cell phone reminded me all hours of the night.

I felt rising hope for the city's future, despite the shadow cast by my predecessor, Ray Nagin, who was convicted on federal charges of bribery, wire fraud, and tax evasion, and sentenced to ten years in prison—the first mayor in New Orleans history so prosecuted. Nevertheless, we had come far in the major rebuilding to make New Orleans better functioning and more livable since Katrina. It had been nine years since 80 percent of the neighborhoods were submerged. I focused on keeping our construction work on time, on task, and under budget, if possible.

The City Charter prohibits a third consecutive term for mayor. I wanted to leave a city truly transformed at the end of my eighth year. By chance, 2018 would mark the city's Tricentennial. I felt the three-hundredth anniversary would provide a rare opportunity to showcase the post-Katrina resurrection and highlight revitalized neighborhoods and the array of the resurgent music, restaurants, and artistic culture. Despite the city's traumatic racial history, New Orleans had a growing international image as the birthplace of jazz and the home of a rich African American culture. In asking civic leaders to form a Tricentennial Commission, I spoke at length with James Carville and Walter Isaacson. I solicited ideas from both of them, and reached out to Wynton Marsalis.

Most people think of Wynton as a jazz musician. I consider Wynton Marsalis a force of nature. We had gone to different high schools but knew each other in passing back then. Wynton was barely twenty when his first album was released and set him on his path as a prolific recording artist. He received the Pulitzer Prize for distinguished musical composition, and he guided the establishment of Jazz at Lincoln Center, which he serves as artistic director. Like his father, Wynton has a commitment to teaching, taking time on his concert tours to lead countless workshops for students.

Wynton Marsalis also reads more than most people I know. In the conversations we'd had over the years I came away impressed by his astute sense of history. Though he lives in New York, I wanted his ideas on the Tricentennial planning, and I wanted to get his commitment to perform as we developed our schedule of events. I also would bend his ear whenever I could on using art as a tool in our fight against violence. I wanted him, as an artist and historian, to curate the Tricentennial year in the same way you would art in a museum. I didn't think this was asking for much, and in return I got something for which I never bargained.

Wynton had a concert in New Orleans not long after my reelection and agreed to a Tricentennial chat. We met at a Starbucks, downtown on Convention Center Boulevard, near his hotel. In the amiable way of one native son to another, I gave a verbal sketch of my plans for the three-hundredth anniversary year and asked him to help.

"I'll do it. But there's something I'd like you to do."

"What's that?"

"Take down the Robert E. Lee statue."

"You lost me on that."

"I don't like the fact that Lee Circle is named Lee Circle."

"Why is that?"

"Let me help you see it through my eyes. Who is he? What does he represent? And in that most prominent space in the city of New Orleans, does that space reflect who we were, who we want to be, or who we are?"

Suddenly I was listening.

"Louis Armstrong left and never came back. He did not even want to be buried in his hometown," he continued. You ever think about what Robert E. Lee means to someone black?"

"Black and white people watch Carnival parades there."

"A big reason so many black people left New Orleans is they didn't feel welcome. You ever think of that African American diaspora?"

I indeed knew that black people had been leaving for

decades to seek better opportunities; still, the city had a 60 percent African American majority. In rebuilding neighborhoods post-flood I was trying to foster a better made and more welcoming city. As he spoke of the symbolic weight of Confederate monuments, Marsalis blindsided me.

"That would be one big political fight, Wynton."

"Yeah, man. But it's the right thing to do. You should think about it."

My head was spinning: *I need to find a way to tell Wynton why I can't do this. The legislature, or Congress, will try to stop me.* This would be a huge political fight. I wasn't sure the juice was worth the squeeze.

But as my wheels kept spinning, the idea of state or federal authorities blocking a mayor on an initiative in his city troubled me. Who controlled the monument? NOPD would respond to any threat to public order at the park or monument itself—city services, city money. As a lawyer, I wanted to know who *owned* the Robert E. Lee monument. As mayor, I wanted to know how the statue went up. Who owned the land? Where did authority lie?

New Orleans has a home rule charter. Founded by the French in 1718, the city shifted to Spanish colonial rule in the 1760s, reverted briefly to France in 1803, and a year later, with the Louisiana Purchase, the city older than America became the U.S. Territory of Orleans. Louisiana achieved statehood in 1812. As one of the oldest cities in the state, the city's home rule charter provided for local autonomy on certain issues that the state or federal government could not easily preempt. My curiosity was mounting about Lee Circle.

I sent a researcher to the main branch of the public library, two blocks from City Hall across Duncan Plaza, for copies of relevant documents from the department that houses the city archives.

Before the Lee statue was erected in 1884, I learned, the space had been called Place du Tivoli for nearly half a century, after the beautiful spaces in Italy outside of Rome and in Paris. In fact, in one of my favorite finds in my research, Tivoli Circle (as it was also known) had been the site of a Union camp in 1864. Although the Lee icon has a commanding presence, Lee himself had virtually no ties to the city. Some records reflect that he visited New Orleans once, very briefly, before the war. He sacrificed a promising military career in the U.S. Army to become general of the Confederate troops. He led the fight to destroy the Union for the purpose of maintaining slavery.

I learned that New Orleans was the largest slave market in America. Fortunes were made in the antebellum era by people who used slaves as collateral for bank loans, and thought little of sundering families at the auction to make a profit. In reviewing the documents my staff had researched, I was intrigued by the historical summary I found in a form for the National Register of Historic Places, which had been filed in 1999 to secure status for the equestrian statue of General Beauregard at the small circle outside City Park. The United States Department of the Interior, through the National Park Service, oversees applications for historic status. The document called the statue Beauregard "one of three major Louisiana monuments representing what is known by historians as 'the Cult of the Lost Cause.'"

Cult of the Lost Cause. Cult. Mmm. The definition of "cult," from the *Merriam-Webster Learner's Dictionary*: "A small religious group that is not part of a larger and more accepted religion and that has beliefs regarded by many people as extreme or dangerous; *a situation in which people admire and care about something or someone very much or too much;* a small group of very devoted supporters or fans." [Italics added.]

I knew from my experiences with two Department of the Interior facilities—Jean Lafitte Park, south of the city in Barataria, and the New Orleans Jazz National Historical Park—that the uniformed rangers were well-read men and women, enriching the lectures and tours they gave; for the Jazz Park they had conducted extensive oral histories of musicians to gain insight for their presentations, educational materials, and programming ideas. The narrative for the National Register of Historic Places application reflected similarly high research standards:

> The Cult of the Lost Cause had its roots in the Southern search for justification and the need to find a substitute for victory in the Civil War. In attempting to deal with defeat, Southerners created an image of the war as a great heroic epic. A major theme of the Cult of the Lost Cause was the clash of two civilizations, one inferior to the other. The North, "invigorated by constant struggle with nature, had become materialistic, grasping for wealth and power." The South had a "more generous climate" which had led to a finer society based upon "veracity and honor in man, chastity and fidelity in women." Like tragic heroes, Southerners had waged a noble but doomed struggle to preserve their superior civilization. There was an element of chivalry in the way the South had fought, achieving noteworthy victories against staggering

odds. This was the "Lost Cause" as the late nineteenth-century saw it, and a whole generation of Southerners set about glorifying and celebrating it.

As I read more about the Lost Cause, I was shocked to realize how much I had not learned about the War Between the States, which is what they called it in courses when I was growing up. The idea made pervasive by Lost Cause adherents—that the war had never been about slavery, but defending regional integrity—shaped the twisted logic of retaliation against African Americans in Reconstruction, culminating in the 1890s, when Louisiana, during a wave of white violence, deprived most blacks of the right to vote. Lynchings became almost commonplace across the South.

In a 2015 *Washington Post* op-ed, James W. Loewen, a retired University of Vermont sociology professor, and the author of *Lies Across America: What Our Historic Sites Get Wrong*, notes:

> The Confederates won with the pen (and the noose) what they could not win on the battlefield: the cause of white supremacy and the dominant understanding of what the war was all about. We are still digging ourselves out from under the misinformation they spread, which has manifested in our public monuments and our history books. The resulting mythology took hold of the nation a generation later and persists—which is why a presidential candidate can suggest, as Michele Bachmann did in 2011, that slavery was somehow pro-family, and why the public, per the Pew Research Center, believes that the war was fought mainly over states' rights.

The bigotry shaped by that myth was hardwired into the thinking of many Southern whites, as I discovered growing up, a century after the Civil War. *Moon the Coon! Your daddy ruined this city!* A generation later, David Duke ran four state-wide campaigns in Louisiana, even as journalists traced the web of ties to Nazis in his past. Although he lost by huge margins, he won a white majority, suggesting how easily they bought into the role of victims of the same federal government that provided national defense, worker safety standards, environmental safeguards, Social Security, and Medicare. Not until Duke went to prison did his base of support measurably shrink. The power of the Lost Cause cult to distort history and rationalize lynching and the trampling of human rights weighed on me as we considered the legal status of the New Orleans monuments.

I later learned from the work of the Southern Poverty Law Center that there were some seven hundred Confederate memorial monuments and statues erected well after the Civil War. According to its research, "two distinct periods saw a significant rise in the dedication of monuments and other symbols. The first began around 1900, amid the period in which states were enacting Jim Crow laws to disenfranchise the newly freed African Americans and re-segregate society. This spike lasted well into the 1920s, a period that saw a dramatic resurgence of the Ku Klux Klan, which had been born in the immediate aftermath of the Civil War. The second spike began in the early 1950s and lasted through the 1960s, as the civil rights movement led to a backlash among segregationists." They still celebrate official Confederate holidays across the South; luckily, not in Louisiana.

It became clearer and clearer that the symbols were intended to send a specific message to African Americans.

In New Orleans, the statues to Lee, Jefferson Davis, and P. G. T. Beauregard were the most visible manifestations of the Lost Cause cult; but the most glaring symbol was an obelisk that had been erected downtown, next to a statue of Henry Clay on the Canal Street neutral ground, near the river, in 1891.

James Loewen called the Liberty Place monument "the most overtly racist icon to white supremacy in the United States." It commemorated the revolt on September 14, 1874, by several thousand white Democrats, seeking to overturn the Republican Reconstruction government. Loewen continues:

> After incendiary speeches, at four in the afternoon about 8,400 whites attacked 3,000 black members of the state militia, 500 mostly white members of the metropolitan police, and 100 other local police officers, all under the command of General James Longstreet. Longstreet had been a Confederate general; indeed, he was Lee's senior corps commander at Gettysburg. After the war, he came to believe, in accord with the Fourteenth and Fifteenth Amendments, that blacks should have full rights as citizens including voting rights.
>
> In fifteen minutes, the White Leaguers routed Longstreet's forces and captured him. Eleven metropolitans and their allies were killed and 60 wounded. Twenty-one White Leaguers were killed including two bystanders, and nineteen were wounded. White League officials then took charge of all state offices in

Louisiana and appealed to [President Ulysses S.] Grant for recognition.

The president instead sent federal troops to restore the constituted government; but the insurrection had a major impact on Congress. In 1877, Reconstruction ended; federal troops left the occupied areas, and the defeated South unleashed a wave of terror against blacks while subjugating them to segregated schools and inferior public education without the right to vote. In 1891, the White League obelisk—that is what I wish to call it from here on, because "liberty" had nothing to do with the White League—was erected on the Canal Street median with the names of White League men who had died. Former mayor William J. Behan, who arranged the installation ceremony, had himself been part of the armed revolt.

This is really specious, I thought. The South lost the war and a group of people got together and decided that they were going to adorn the city with monuments that revered those who fought on behalf of a cause that was lost, which they wanted to make seem noble. They were fighting for the right to own and sell black human beings.

Now, I'm a white guy from the South, through and through; but those icons are not speaking for me. Who were they speaking for? A small and very determined minority. Take an honest review of our history: the South wasn't all white. New Orleans was a huge slave market and the city was filled with slaveholders, but we had a multicultural community even back then, including a large population of free people of color, who could vote and were citizens. In fact, the city of New Orleans from the moment of its birth had been incredibly diverse. So who was exercising political authority? William Behan, who put up the Liberty Monument, had been a Confederate soldier.

As I read more about the Lost Cause, I concluded that the statues were a lie. Their advocates had stolen the identity of New Orleans.

The Civil War began in 1861, with General Beauregard of New Orleans leading the charge against Fort Sumter, a federal seaport in Charleston, South Carolina. New Orleans fell early to the Union, in April 1862, and as an occupied city through the war was not a hotbed of Rebel revolts. Behan was a member of the elite Pickwick Club; the White League met at the Boston Club, which for generations had a viewing stand where Rex, the king of Mardi Gras, toasted his young queen, a debutante of the season. Boston Club members supported Behan, and in 1874 took the law into their own hands in the White League revolt, wealthy men resorting to vigilante violence, trying to topple a Republican administration. Behan was part of the society that essentially hijacked the image of a city whose racial and cultural diversity fascinated memoirists and travel writers before and after the war.

The resurgence of white power, enshrined in the 1891 erection of the White League obelisk, had long-lasting impact through the twentieth century. It kept black children out of good schools; it kept black citizens out of jobs; it condemned them to poor housing, terrible health care, and poverty. And I again recalled, many talented African Americans simply left the city. *Louis Armstrong left. He even refused to be buried here.*

My education came late, but it caught up with me in a hurry.

We can be proud of our ancestors who served the

Confederacy as men who fought courageously for a cause larger than themselves. We can also recognize that in the context of history they were wrong. Which is to say they were human.

Slavery was the reason for the war, and as we learn in unblinkered histories, Southerners protecting their "traditional" way of life committed horrendous moral crimes against people of African descent. And yet, in 1884, when the Lee statue was installed, the *Daily Picayune* captured a mind-set of prevailing power: "We cannot ignore the fact that the secession has been stigmatized as treason and that the purest and bravest men in the South have been denounced as guilty of shameful crime. By every application of literature and art, we must show to all coming ages that with us, at least, there dwells no sense of guilt." The Cult of the Lost Cause succeeded.

I decided that this sanitizing of history must end. The monuments do not represent history, nor the soul of New Orleans. They were not tools for teaching. Instead, they were the product of a warped political movement by wealthy people supporting a mayor who was determined to regain power for white people, to reduce blacks to second-class status, and to control how history was seen, read, and accepted by whites. As the mayor of this multicultural city, trying to rebuild not as it was but the way it should always have been, I concluded that Wynton was right. They should come down. They are not of our age, nor of our making, and they deserve no prominence in our city.

So here I am in my second term, thinking, if anyone can get rid of those symbols it's me. A future African American mayor would face an excruciating struggle with this because of the way power and money undulate in this city—it would turn into an ugly referendum on race with the voices of a sentimental South that stands on whitewashed history raising a protest about heritage and honor, not slavery. I thought my team was good enough to bring people together to achieve a reconciliation, a way of putting the past to rest. Should we really be debating the Civil War in 2017?

Something else was digging at me. If William Behan, who was mayor from 1882 to 1884, and participated in erecting a monument in 1891, did something that insults and demeans a great portion of my citizens, then it is my responsibility as mayor to course-correct and challenge that version of history that prominent scholars have found specious: the notion of a chivalrous South that lost the war for noble reasons. Many claim that many white Southerners went off to war in the belief that they had to defend their homeland; but it was the politicians and their generals who determined whether a war should be fought and why. Alexander H. Stephens, the vice president of the Confederate States, in a March 21, 1861, speech at Macon, Georgia, said of the "new government," the Southern states, "its foundations are laid, its corner-stone rests, upon the great truth that the negro is not equal to the white man; that slavery subordination to the superior race is his natural and normal condition. This, our new government, is the first, in the history of the world, based upon this great physical, philosophical, and moral truth. . . . With us, all of the white race, however high or low, rich or poor, are equal in the eye of the law. Not so with the negro. Subordination is his place. He, by nature, or by the curse against Canaan, is fitted for that condition which he occupies in our system."

The Union led by President Lincoln did not want a slave economy, and prevailed in the war over that issue. But winning the war hardly settled the matter or secured equality and opportunity for black Americans. Reconstruction turned into a nightmare of terrorism against black people by Southern white potentates. Reconstruction eventually gave us the statues.

While I am processing a lot of this information, I am also thinking legally. For a short period of time I am the steward of a government that began in 1718. I am a lawyer, and the research by my staff, and the City Attorney, is conclusive: The city government had control over that property. Behan put up that Liberty Place monument, and I could take it down. In truth, the White League obelisk had become an embarrassment even to many whites. When the black-majority City Council in 1993 declared it a public nuisance and ordered it removed, it precipitated a legal appeal from die-hard traditionalists in federal court under the false guise of historical preservation. The upshot was that the city moved the obelisk from its prominent place on Canal Street to an obscure spot, behind the Aquarium of the Americas, next to a parking garage.

My city budget had to pay again and again to clean antiracist graffiti off the White League monument, a symbol that flaunted the constitutional principle of equal protection under the law. City ordinances reflect the evolution of a government, its constituents, and their needs. The City Council under the New Orleans Code had defined a public nuisance:

> The thing honors, praises or fosters ideologies which are in conflict with the requirements of equal protection for citizens as provided by the constitution and laws of the United States, the state, or the laws of the city and gives honor or praise to those who participated in the killings of public employees of the city

or the state or suggests the supremacy of one ethnic, religious or racial group over any other, or gives honor or praise to any violent actions taken wrongfully against citizens of the city to promote ethnic, religious, or racial supremacy of any group over another.

It was clear to me that this spoke directly to the monuments, and that the city's authority over its public spaces took precedence over a designation of national historic significance; we could remove the statues of Lee, Davis, Beauregard, and the White League under this ordinance. I would need the support of a majority of the seven-member City Council; I felt that if I laid the political groundwork, we could achieve this. We were in early 2015 now. I thought about how beautiful it would be to have a fountain with a swirl of colors atop the sixty-foot column to supplant the icon of General Lee— we would send out a request for proposals to distinguished sculptors and artists, appoint a blue-ribbon committee to choose the design, and with enough lead time, we would have a world-class monument by 2018, during the Tricentennial events.

New Orleans has always been more progressive than most Southern cities by virtue of diversity and our festive culture, centered around Carnival in winter and Jazz & Heritage Festival in the spring. Whites are a voting minority, but there is a cordiality in civic affairs as the eccentric, colorful nature of the town draws residents to the proverbial public square with a passion for the city as a unique place, one that puts a great premium on enjoying life.

I realized that for many whites, Lee Circle was a place that had always been there, a familiar piece of the urban fabric, a landmark, like streetcars, with the small park around the base of the monument where people navigated bad traffic patterns and watched Mardi Gras parades. As tolerant as New Orleanians are in many respects, I knew that a move to change the traditional cityscape would involve a good deal of retail politics. Call on key people, brief them, generate support for the plan.

One of the first people I spoke with about taking down the Robert E. Lee statue was my father. Moon Landrieu was in his mideighties, an active walker around Audubon Park; he and my mother still lived in the house I grew up in on Prieur Street with several grandchildren in residence while they're in law school or college. I briefed him on what I wanted to do. "Son, I'm not sure I'd do that," he said gently. "That would be a big fight." He was speaking to me as a father, concerned for my career and future. I sensed that he understood the importance of removing Confederate icons but was concerned about the personal and political fallout on me.

I love my father but I was on a determined course. And I had a sneaking suspicion that he would do the same thing if he were standing in my shoes at this moment. I was raised at his knee and I know him as well as he knows me. This was the guy who in 1960 was one of only two white legislators to vote against a powerful segregationist package. And so I ignored his parental advice.

What did Robert E. Lee, who allegedly spent one night in New Orleans, actually *do for this city*, compared to Louis Armstrong, Fats Domino, Tennessee Williams, the Marsalis family, the Neville family, Anne Rice—how many names do I need?

The Civil War was about slavery. And Robert E. Lee was being celebrated in our most prominent spaces. Whenever I had second thoughts, I went back to two numbers.

Six million. Six hundred fifteen thousand.

Six million is the approximate number of human beings who were enslaved in our exceptional country until 1865. Six million. Look at it and say it again. You can see it. You can see them. These six million included men, women, children. Many of whom were beaten, raped, tortured. Hung like fruit. Forced to work against their will. Their families torn apart.

Six hundred fifteen thousand is the number of soldiers who died in the war that we waged against ourselves. Feel this number deeply. One side to save the nation and end slavery. The other to destroy the nation as we knew it and to preserve slavery. No one was left unscarred. The first shot of the Civil War was fired on Fort Sumter on April 12, 1861, by Confederate soldiers under the command of P. G. T. Beauregard. His future general was Robert E. Lee and their self-proclaimed president was Jefferson Davis. They fought against the United States of America to preserve the institution of slavery. They lost. But six hundred fifteen thousand Americans also lost their lives in this fight to preserve the Union.

Six million human beings were enslaved in our country. The largest number of those human beings were sold into slavery in my city, New Orleans. There is good and evil. Right and wrong. Truth and falsehood. The false narrative that has taken hold, a perpetual state of denial that has been left unchecked, has strangled the South that I love and made us weaker as a nation.

In hindsight, I wished I had explained it in terms more Southerners might understand better—SEC football. The

Civil War was not an LSU versus Alabama game. The Confederacy wasn't just a game with each side suiting up in their jerseys for the weekend. It was a war to keep slavery. There should be no doubt that the Confederacy was on the wrong side of humanity and history. As a country, we ought to be at the point now, in the year 2018, where we can recognize the basic truth that slavery was wrong, accept it, and figure out the appropriate way to remember it—but not to revere it.

I wanted to get in touch with major figures from all communities who had supported me in the past and seek their backing for a fountain to replace the Lee statue. The first person I visited was a white businesswoman and philanthropist in New Orleans. As she sat listening, I explained the genesis of my project, the conversation with Wynton, and the due diligence I had made the city undergo in determining legal ownership of the spaces. She did not warm to the idea. In conveying her position, she never raised her voice or said an angry word. She probably could have stopped the project had she taken a stance of militant opposition, begun making calls, and spoken out in public. She did not, and I am grateful for that. She was gracious, but I left the meeting feeling pretty low.

I called Walter Isaacson and recounted my discussions both with her and with Wynton. "I agree with Wynton," said Isaacson. "They ought to come down—the monuments don't really represent New Orleans."

"I cannot do this by myself. You guys are going to have to speak up publicly." He said he would; both Isaacson and Marsalis eventually wrote op-ed pieces backing my decision.

I called Ken Burns, director of the PBS series *The Civil War*, which had taught so many about the realities of that war. I told him what I had learned, the dilemma I faced, and asked if I was off-course. "No," said Burns, "I think you're on the right track."

Actually, I was moving along two tracks—sounding out people involved in the Tricentennial planning, and meeting with financial supporters of my campaigns and major projects for New Orleans, hoping to generate a budget to build a fountain after General Lee's statue was taken down.

On March 18, 2015, I gathered the Tricentennial's executive committee and top historians on New Orleans. The Tricentennial's historical and cultural advisory committee included Sybil Morial, who had been first lady of New Orleans when the late Dutch Morial was mayor; historian Lawrence N. Powell (*The Accidental City*); Freddi Williams Evans (*Congo Square*); geographer Richard Campanella of Tulane University; Dr. Ibrahima Seck, academic director of the museum of slavery, Whitney Heritage Plantation Corporation; Carol Bebelle of the Ashé Cultural Arts Center; and Priscilla Lawrence, executive director of the Historic New Orleans Collection, among several others. They were joined by the chairs of other Tricentennial committees, from finance to marketing to community engagement. It was as diverse as such a group could be.

After updates on a few projects and books and a general lesson on New Orleans history, including discussions on the slave trade, Reconstruction, the *Plessy* decision, and other key moments in New Orleans history, we moved into a discussion of how we want the outside world to view New Orleans at its three-hundredth year and how we could use the Tricentennial to move the city forward, almost as an organizing event, like you would do with an Olympics. It was all a lead-in to what I knew was going to be a sensitive topic, to put it mildly. A few minutes into my remarks, I recounted part of the conversation

I'd had with Wynton. I noted that symbols matter and that I wanted to take down the Robert E. Lee statue. An audible gasp went up in the room; I am not sure how many people were in that chorus, but as I recounted the steps I had taken since Wynton's request, it surprised me to see a few African Americans who thought it not worth the bother, and a sprinkling of whites who liked the idea. But the opinions ranged widely.

One of the first to speak up said she might be for taking down the Lee statue, but that it could "overshadow a lot of our work."

"That statue doesn't bother me," said another African American woman; she didn't think blacks were that concerned about it.

As people weighed in with intelligent comments, pro and con, another African American businesswoman offered some thoughts. A New Orleans native who had moved away for work, she hadn't given much thought to the Lee icon until her young daughter was in town with her one time to visit family. As they were driving along St. Charles Avenue, the girl said, "What's that statue up there?"

"Robert E. Lee."

"Mama, who is that?"

"The general who led the Confederates in the Civil War."

"Well, was he fighting for me?"

"No, he wasn't. He was fighting to keep people slaves."

"Then why is he up there?"

The recollection of that conversation really hit me. As the meeting continued, with people suggesting that instead of taking down, we *simply add things*: A statue, for example, to civil rights leader Oretha Castle Haley on the avenue now named for her in Central City. A plaque that might put the statue in context. These were solid, committed people, people as good as they come in any city, wrestling with an idea I had delivered out of nowhere (just as Wynton had done to me), and yet what came home to me through this candid discussion was that no one said, *I demand that the Lee statue stay where it is.* People debated, disagreed, but preservation of the Lost Cause was not on anyone's plate. But it was the story of that little girl that stayed with me because Wynton had asked me to think of it through the eyes of an African American. And now I had heard about a young African American girl trying to make sense out of this statue in one of our most prominent places. That pretty much did it for me. Because I was clear that my job as mayor was to prepare this city for that young girl's future. So I locked in.

Four of my five children were grown and out of the house by then; none yet married, we had no grandchildren. God willing, a grandbaby or more will come. I began to think of what I would say to that grandson or granddaughter, years from now, who said, "Paw Paw, when you were mayor, what did you think of Robert E. Lee? Why didn't you take that statue down?" I knew I wouldn't be able to look that child in the face. I imagined her saying, "You had the power. You knew that slavery was wrong, and you didn't do it. Why?"

The distortion of the past was getting under my skin. I made appointments with several of the wealthiest citizens in town, supporters of my past campaigns, including friends of my father, each a contributor to the public good. Laying out the history of Tivoli Circle before Robert E. Lee reached the perch, and my plan for a world-class fountain for a renamed circle after the statue's removal, I met a series of stares. One by one. Even liberals were uneasy with the move. I left those meetings discouraged, wondering again if I was on the wrong track.

On June 17, 2015, the massacre of nine people praying at Emanuel African Methodist Episcopal Church in Charleston, South Carolina, left me stunned. A high school dropout and white supremacist goes into a house of worship to murder reverent people because of their color. My mind races back to the bombing in Birmingham. To the over four thousand lynchings in the South. To *Plessy v. Ferguson*. The line is clear and direct. I thought, *This is never going to stop.*

Do not tell me that this man's pathology is not linked to Lost Cause myopia, which allowed generations of white Southerners to deny the acts of indecency and inhumanity perpetrated on black people. After so much progress made since the civil rights movement, what kind of country are we becoming? Are black people still, now, open targets in the South? As the sorrow and anger sank into me, I doubled down in my conviction that the Robert E. Lee icon must come down—*and* the statue of Jefferson Davis, *and* Beauregard, *and* get the godforsaken White League obelisk, obscured behind the aquarium, off public ground once and forever. We cannot change the past, but we are not obligated to cave in to some nostalgia-coated idea that a statue is good because it's old. Symbols matter. And these were symbols of white supremacy put up for a particular reason.

I was not exactly stunned when the Louisiana Landmarks Society, a historic preservation group, released hostile comments after a meeting of historians who were uneasy about the removal of statuary from an era of Louisiana history. The Foundation for Historical Louisiana in Baton Rouge opposed what we wanted to do as well, but then again, it opposes everything. I knew people in both groups and understood their aesthetic concerns in the abstract; but the reality was that moving a statue from one place of prominence to a museum or park is a change in geography, not a form of destruction. It is also change with a message. We don't want this work in this place, because of the dehumanizing message it sends to people of color, many of whom are the descendants of slaves. *We must draw that line as a statement of civilization*, that we have advanced in a moral sense to embrace ideas of liberty and justice. We cannot change events before our time but must view the past with an honest viewfinder lest we ignore the great moral injustice that brought us into this dispute.

I felt emboldened when South Carolina governor Nikki Haley and Charleston mayor Joe Riley (one of my mentors), in the wake of the Charleston massacre, decided to remove the Confederate flag from its position atop the State Capitol. A Republican and Democrat standing shoulder to shoulder. News coverage had shown the young killer posing with a Rebel flag license plate and other racist symbols. The horrific murders, whose victims included State Senator Clementa Pinckney, a man much respected across the aisle, drove a shift among South Carolina lawmakers who lined up behind Haley and Riley.

In May 2014, long before I'd started thinking about monuments, I had launched Welcome Table New Orleans, an initiative focused on race, reconciliation, and community with a cross-section of civic leaders meeting on a regular basis. Now, at the first anniversary celebration of the Welcome Table, as groups presented their projects, I sidled up to the edge of the stage. I apologized for wrongs that had been committed in New Orleans, specifically slavery. And I said that on this day, we should start to think about and discuss taking down the Lost Cause monuments.

In a matter of days, New Orleans ministers, white and black, voiced their support. I didn't have the establishment behind me; but the many religious leaders gave me a surge of hope, particularly Shawn Anglim, a white pastor of First Grace United Methodist Church, which stood catty-corner to the Jefferson Davis statue on Canal Street. The church had a sign outside with "Take Down Jeff Davis Monument" on one side and "Black Lives Matter" on the other. Pastor Antoine Barriere, Pastor Charles Southall, the Reverend Marie Galatas, and so many others offered prayers, public support, and strong moral voice to the cause. They would have my back.

The city of New Orleans has a clear process to follow in order to remove a monument. The Mayor's Office, the chief administrative officer, and the superintendent of police must concur that it constitutes a public nuisance before the documentation can be presented to the Human Relations Commission and the Historic District Landmark Commission. The White League statue would also need approval from the Vieux Carre Commission, which oversees historic preservation in the French Quarter, where the statue technically stood. CAO Andy Kopplin and Police Chief Michael Harrison embraced my position; the three commissions held long and widely attended public hearings and voted favorably. On September 11, 2015, City Attorney Sharonda Williams submitted a lengthy memorandum and dossier of materials to the City Council, whose support was pivotal.

The hearings were pretty boisterous, even by New Orleans standards, with heckling and jeering from those who opposed the plan (one disgruntled opponent was ejected by police after giving the middle finger to certain members of the audience); but as various people spoke before the seven councilmembers,

I felt our presentation was solid, on legal and moral terms. The most powerful speaker, I thought, was a Lakeview resident, Richard Westmoreland, a retired Marine Corps lieutenant colonel, who said that Robert E. Lee was a great general, but compared him to Erwin Rommel, the World War II German tank commander. There are no statues of Rommel in Germany, he continued. "They are ashamed. The question is, why aren't we?" Westmoreland said. "Make no mistake, slavery was the great sin of this nation." In a letter to the *New Orleans Advocate*, Westmoreland wrote:

> The "heritage" argument doesn't stand the test of time. These men were traitors. We are the United States before we are the South. How can anyone begin to think that these remembrances aren't offensive and disrespectful to African Americans? They are offensive to me as a retired military officer. They are offensive to me as a citizen; our tax money maintains these sites. Their existence is offensive to me as a human being; the monuments to the Confederacy on our public lands are disrespectful at best. They are subtle, government-sanctioned racism.
>
> There is nothing about our "heritage" with the Confederacy worthy of embracing. We are not who we once were. We should be proud of that. We are our brother's keeper. I am white, by the way, a fact that shouldn't be relevant in this argument, but we know it still is.

A week before Christmas 2015, the City Council voted 6–1 in favor of dismantling monuments. We then began our procurement process, the term used for finding and negotiating with contractors for the work specified on city projects. Meanwhile, the Louisiana Landmarks Society filed suit against our plan, citing its members' "recognized interest in the aesthetic and cultural well-being in the city of New Orleans, and in the preservation and maintenance of the four monuments at issue." The lawsuit, whose petitioners included the Foundation for Historical Louisiana, Beauregard Camp No. 130, and a group called Monumental Task Committee, claimed that taking the structures down violated their First Amendment right to free expression, "which they exercise by maintaining and preserving the historic character and nature of the city of New Orleans, including their monuments."

I was sure that we had taken the proper steps in what, for me, was in its most simple form a property rights issue: who has authority over monuments on city land? The preservationists and their allies asked the federal court to overrule the city on an issue of its own governance. In good faith, I advised the judge that the city would take no action until the dispute was resolved, something I foolishly did not foresee taking long. Meanwhile, my staff and I were in dialogue with various construction companies that routinely bid for contracted work on city projects. With the FEMA funds we had obtained, combined with other support streams, New Orleans had at least a billion dollars in work ongoing. One prominent citizen called me and pledged $170,000 for the removal costs, predicated on anonymity, allowing me to say that city funds would not be expended for the work.

A Baton Rouge company that had done work for the city of New Orleans agreed to service the order for removing the structure once we were out of the legal thicket. I assumed the legal appeals would be tossed out soon; before we reached that point, the owner and his wife received death threats, which we reported to the FBI, and his expensive sports car was set afire in the driveway of his business.

The spread of domestic terrorism has many small stories like this, threats, acts of religious desecration, and vandalism that move across the news radar or make a few paragraphs on inside pages of the local press, and no one gets caught, or if so quite some time later. This is part of the ho-hum racism that eats through our country every day. In other words, we really haven't made it as far as we like to think—we're still mired in a mentality where *they* could lynch you, destroy your reputation, hurt your business, or engage in symbolic lynchings, like a cross burned on your lawn or the car in your driveway torched. When the media reported the story on the burned car, I realized we were facing an opposition that went far beyond historic preservationists to a burning fringe of people bent on criminal behavior.

As tension built inside me, a thought kept gnawing at me—how badly we had been taught about the Civil War, how little about slavery or Reconstruction, or Jim Crow, for that matter. Also how the ingrained racial attitudes I encountered in youth and through adulthood in a city with such a wonderful mix of humanity reflected in the music and cuisine, the balls and parades, nevertheless had a cold, dark underside—and it's not just New Orleans. You can drive fifty miles from here and find people in rural towns who felt emotionally invested in the Robert E. Lee statue *as an idea of the Civil War—what the South was.* Drive a few hundred more miles to outer edges of the South and find white people who think "the South" is misunderstood, that the heritage of their ancestors, or the idea of an honorable war, as taught in schools and passed through family tradition, supersedes *why that war was fought.*

How else do we explain the blanket of hostility toward black people that shrouds the voting patterns of the white South? Has the white South truly reckoned with the Civil War? Think about the Southern Strategy of the Republican Party as fomented by Nixon, carried on by Reagan, and now reenacted with Trump. Even with large black populations, no Southern state has a voting black majority; and every Southern state is schizophrenically split on voting lines of race, Louisiana high among them. Race is the great dividing wedge used by what was once the party of Lincoln to attract working-class whites and country-club conservatives who otherwise share few economic interests with each other but are united against the interests of African Americans.

I went through agony in those months of delays. A lot of people in this town who could have spoken in favor of my position kept silent. The issue had become so hot and controversial, I was somewhat isolated from most of my former white supporters and allies. The job became more lonely. I can fault myself for failing to anticipate the ferocity of the opposition, but I didn't expect that people would be so animated by the heresy of what I proposed that it would take a year and a half of appeals and litigation that went through five courts and thirteen—yes, *thirteen*—judges, all the way to the U.S. Fifth Circuit Court of Appeals, which today has become the most conservative appellate court in the United States. This is the same court where the venerable Judge John Minor Wisdom, an Eisenhower Republican who lived off St. Charles Avenue, Uptown, and in my opinion is one of the absolute saints of American jurisprudence, issued his legendary order to desegregate the University of Mississippi in 1962. Courts change as the politics of a region change, but the U.S. Fifth Circuit affirmed our authority to proceed. Indeed, the city of New Orleans had the right to remove statues on its own public property that authorities of the city deemed a public nuisance.

As the public temperature rose, the benefactor who offered to cover the cost of removing the statues called with a change of heart: He couldn't be associated with the project because if anyone should learn about his role, "I'll get run out of town." The year-and-a-half delay caused by the lawsuits, coupled with the burning of the first contractor's car and threats to him and his wife, had a chain reaction, and the contractors who did city work pulled back.

Now I faced an issue that I had never anticipated: how to physically get the monuments down. With hundreds of millions of dollars in city projects, supported by the funds we had arduously negotiated from FEMA and other federal agencies to rebuild New Orleans, and with crews on job sites across the city, *I can't get anyone to lease me a damned crane!* This still eats at me: of all the billions of dollars we'd spent on contractors in this town, I couldn't find one company with the conviction to say, "This is city business; therefore we should handle it." But the fear that the construction company owners felt was a reality we had to confront. And it wasn't just in Louisiana; we had called across the country. It was as if this project were blacklisted.

The Confederate monument partisans found a couple of brave members of the Louisiana legislature willing to declare all military monuments historically sacrosanct, putting Rebel soldiers in the Civil War on equal footing with GIs who fought against the Nazis in World War II.

For all the chest beating in Baton Rouge, the federal courts did not bend their position as the appeals wore on. By the middle of 2016, as the lawsuits ate up the time and energy of my legal staff, not to mention city funds, Homeland Security and the NOPD were advising us to take extraordinary precautions as we inched toward the inevitable point when we would be free and clear to take the structures down. Protests at the statue sites were escalating. By late September 2016, outside agitators were a regular presence. David Duke even made a spectacle by counterprotesting a march to Jackson Square. We had hundreds of police brought in to keep the peace. There were only seven arrests after several minor fights broke out.

As we moved through 2016 and the early part of 2017, with the opponents' appeals running out of steam, we anticipated protesters on both sides of the issue to show up with banners, raised voices, and some alt-right figures carrying firearms. We were no longer dealing with a political dispute; this had become a security crisis.

In City Hall, the Mayor's Office switchboard faced a tide of belligerent callers. Our receptionists who took pride in their courtesy to callers were subjected to profanities, and threatening words, which the system was taping, the worst of which we shared with federal law enforcement. Despite the many other things that involved our time in running the city, the swell of hostilities created a siege mentality that wore on all of us. As we mapped supremely careful plans for the final push, I went home many evenings depressed about the worst impulses of a backward, bigoted South spilling into the city and my life. At home, Cheryl and I received obscene calls, just as my parents had in the 1970s when Dad was desegregating the city work force.

We felt the cold shoulders, the averted eye contact and gazes elsewhere by some neighbors and certain people we thought were friends. I had one of the most startling experiences while I was riding my bike in the park early each morning. I would be yelled at consistently by the same woman. One particular Sunday, it was more vicious and nasty than normal. You can imagine my surprise when a few hours later Cheryl and I were at Mass and I saw her giving out Communion—she was a eucharistic minister. It was surreal. People who had served for years on civic boards quit. Even now, at a distance of nearly a year, I cannot forget the pain we felt, nor how hard it was on some days to get through breakfast, for all the hatred sent our way, or for the deep, mean chill we felt when we entered a room for a public event. But when I got down, my thoughts always turned to the picture of John Lewis, at just twenty-three years old, standing tall at the foot of the Edmund Pettus Bridge, knowing he was about to get beat up by that sheriff. And then I kept going, knowing full well his burden was much heavier than mine.

The harassment got personal as well. The way they hang you politically in the South is to accuse you of having black blood. It was something that scares people to death. Passe blanc, or "pass for white," is age-old, so it was no surprise or shock to me that our political enemies would try to discredit me, my father, or my sister with this threat or accusation. Maybe I didn't know enough to be afraid, or maybe I could have cared less if I had black blood. Honestly, I would consider it a badge of honor. So when they dug up some records of my grandfather, Joseph Geoffrey Landrieu—you know, the patient one, the one who untangled my fishing line, the one who loved me so much, and the one who dropped dead in front of me—and said, "he had black blood," it didn't embarrass me in the least. He was one of the nicest, most decent people I ever knew.

But the accusation is insidious anyway. Why does one have to have black blood to see that the Confederacy was wrong about history and humanity? Why does one have to have any kind of particular blood to recognize human hatred or misery or unkindness? This, though, is the kind of thinking that was so ferocious on the other side.

Eventually, the State House bills to thwart our project failed to pass the Senate committee, and the clock was ticking on the final decision by the federal appeals court. I am thankful to the courageous legislators and senators who helped. Confederate statue sympathizers were holding candlelight vigils at the monuments to the generals. A racially diverse group called Take 'Em Down NOLA, which wanted every street name, park, or statue associated with slave owning removed or renamed, was marching and mounting protests. Many of their principals had been involved in the movement for several decades.

In early May, vandals spray-painted slogans on the base of the Lee monument: *Memory never dies . . . White Supremacy is a Lie . . . Take it down now."* There were other ominous signs from the opposition. As the city's authority was finally resolved by the federal court, we knew that white supremacist alt-right groups would be heading to New Orleans.

We put the removal bid documents out once and for all. We had to protect the identities of those who downloaded them. In the end, a single African American contractor gave a bid of six hundred thousand dollars for the removal of the three larger monuments, predicated on law enforcement protection. Another city contractor said it could still move forward with the obelisk. The city accepted the bid, which was four times what we had originally budgeted, but understandable given the torching of the previous company owner's car, an event that had been well covered in the media. Here we were, more than a half century after white mob attacks on civil rights leaders in Selma, Alabama, and a city lawfully preparing to move three statues and an obelisk had become a flashpoint in America's worsening racial crisis. How far we have come since those days in the 1960s. Yes, how far we have come—and how far we must go to see the fires of racial hatred ebb.

On the advice of Police Chief Michael Harrison and Homeland Security director Aaron Miller, I decided to dismantle the White League obelisk first, as it had the thinnest base of white support; we did it late at night on the advice of law enforcement to reduce the risk of attack on the workers. It would have made for nice symbolism on a sunny spring day, a contrast of the South, old and new, for TV news to show the White League icon coming down amid the rollout for the Jazz & Heritage Festival, which celebrates the rich diversity of our culture. That was not a chance I wanted to take. The operation began at two in the morning on April 24, 2017. The police SWAT team had sharpshooters in strategic perches with K-9 units circulating to insure the workers' safety. Men driving the trucks, operating equipment, and other workers wore bulletproof vests, helmets, and face masks to guard their anonymity. Cardboard covered the company name on the vehicles and the license plates. All this, to take down an icon to white supremacy! From law enforcement authorities we learned that some people in the crowd were using high-definition cameras, and hovering drones to take pictures, trying to identify the company and the actual individuals who were working. The obelisk was removed in several pieces, with the base of the structure put into a truck and moved to a city storage facility. One down, three to go. I do not smile over the composition of these words.

Most Americans think of white nationalists as crude racists who show up at protests in their Nazi or KKK regalia; that is one reality, but the FBI and Southern Poverty Law Center track these groups because they amass military arsenals as one piece in the larger puzzle of domestic terrorism. As the city offered bids for other contractors on the three statues, the companies on our list received escalating threats. Think of this. If you own a supermarket, a sports bar, a restaurant, or a car dealership, and people start demanding money for protection, the legal term is extortion—being squeezed by criminals for protection money. We protect you so you can do your business. The opposite of this is threats to people who in good faith want to do their business: a contractor hired to take down a city monument is doing a job, not making a political statement. Companies with heavy equipment move and remove all kinds of things. When they get threatened before a job, it's a form of extortion: if you pull out, you won't be hurt, your car won't be torched, no need to worry about your wife or kids.

What the old-line preservationists could not achieve in court, the Nazi, Klan and white power radicals—under that proverbial "shroud of secrecy"—partially achieved by threats of criminal assaults.

As threats persisted following Liberty Place, our law enforcement leadership realized that we needed Homeland Security support in order to thwart the white nationalists determined to sabotage the work of construction companies filling an order by the city of New Orleans. We had five contractors, based on their solid record of delivering work on past contracts, on a standby basis for minor construction projects. We used a different contractor for the Liberty Place removal, and within days that company began receiving threats. We knew we were being monitored by white nationalists—this is terrorism by any other name, despite what President Trump is too cowardly to say about one part of his "base." We had to regroup logistically.

We needed major security assistance in a company that also had connections to provide the contracting work *and a crane*. When you think of what city governance means, how cities build and grow, the idea that a mayor with a work contract, backed by the federal courts, and a record of paying at least $1 billion for city projects, *couldn't get a crane to remove symbols of white power*, what does this say about the country that defeated the Nazi war machine under Hitler? Why have we fallen so far? Where did America get lost?

To get that crane, I turned to outside help. I brought in a Texas-based consulting company with a solid record of providing security and intelligence service for the private sector and the U.S. government in some of the most dangerous places around the world. They were tasked with coordinating with federal, state, and local law enforcement to strengthen protection for the trucks, drivers, crane operators, and other workers doing the removal. They also arranged for companies outside of Louisiana to do the work for which we were unable to contract with local or in-state firms. The simple removal costs should have been about $200,000. We ended up spending $1 million in public funds on security, about five times as much as the entire process of dismantling and removing the monuments would have originally cost. This could have been handled over several months in 2015 at a fraction of the cost had we not faced the lawsuits and the white terrorists. We spent another $1 million in private funds on the actual removal themselves.

We learned through the security firm's operatives that alt-right groups had established safe houses in New Orleans, where they were storing weapons. As we made plans to dismantle the Jefferson Davis statue, the site became a magnet both for white power advocates and for Take 'Em Down NOLA activists. On May 2, a group of Confederate partisans, openly armed, gathered at the Jefferson Davis statue, trading verbal fire with Antifa activists who wanted the statues removed. The police arrested five people, defusing the violence, and erected barricades around the statue, gradually restricting the available space for protest.

But those encounters and new waves of militiamen and alt-right outsiders escalated the threat of violence further, so much so that the FBI offered new guidance, assessing it was "very likely that out-of-state entities, with alleged nexus to domestic terrorist groups, are heading to New Orleans" for a major protest. Alt-right groups and organizations like League of the South were deeming the event the "New Battle of New Orleans." Though tense, NOPD's work with the outside firm and the FBI paid off. There were very few incidents of violence and the monument-removal proponents outnumbered the other side. It was a small victory and also showed what we were really dealing with.

A few days later, on May 11, a day short of the 152nd anniversary of Jeff Davis's capture in 1865, the city removed the Davis statue. As Chelsea Brasted of NOLA.com/*Times-Picayune* reported:

When the monument was first dedicated Feb. 22, 1911, the ceremony included a "living Confederate flag" comprised of public school students, according to the *Times-Picayune*'s report at the time. The paper detailed the event before it took place, noting "the exact cost of the monument will probably never be made public," but that the "money outlay approximates $20,000." Adjusted for inflation, that number would be nearly $500,000 in 2017.

Six days later, the city took down the statue of General P. G. T. Beauregard on his horse, stationed in the small circular space just outside the entrance to City Park. Of the four monuments designated for removal, Beauregard was the most problematic. In his later years, after the war, he had become a reconciling presence, trying to help bring blacks into government, a position that caused him some ostracism before he died. He had actual ties to New Orleans. But the move to memorialize him, well after his death, ignored the latter-day liberal Beauregard to hoist the commanding Rebel general Beauregard, leader of Confederate soldiers, onto a marble horse, hijacked into a symbol of the Lost Cause.

Terence Blanchard, who had passed that statue many times on his way to school, was just coming back from a concert tour when he learned of the statue going down, and went to City Park with his wife, Robin, and their two daughters. He took pictures on his iPhone. "This is something I never thought I'd see in my lifetime," he told a reporter. "It's a sign that the world is changing."

As we moved toward the final step, removing Robert E. Lee from the large white column at the streetcar circle, protests escalated.

By May 2017, I had resigned myself to the reality that my original dream of installing some new piece of unifying artwork or a fountain of the highest aesthetic standards in place of the departed general would never happen before I left office. The legal delays, the white terrorists' threats to contractors, the need to hire the outside security firm, the tense work we had done to allow activists their civil rights, while working hard to defuse violence, all the added expense, the frustrating delays, security issues, and then the wrenching impact of these events on my family and me, taken together, left me glad for what we had achieved, but disappointed that the beauty of the circle I had envisioned for the city would not be mine to execute. I leave this to future city leaders to finish this important work.

In the weeks leading up to the dismantling of the Lee statue, I decided it was time to explain publicly, in a speech, why I had taken this course, to give the people of New Orleans some grasp of the history behind the monuments and to set forth my position that symbols really matter, that they explain a lot about who we are as people. I have given hundreds of speeches without notes and am comfortable in that improvisational mode; but I wanted these words to capture the memories, nuances in life, and stories of other people that brought me to this point. I wanted to give people a deep insight into what political power at its best can do, and the chance that democracy gives us to achieve change for the betterment of society.

The speech was set for the afternoon of May 17 at Gallier Hall, the old City Hall where Jefferson Davis had actually laid in state. Surely by late in the day, I figured, we'd have had the Lee statue removed. As I finished the speech, I learned that the statue had not yet come down. Gallier Hall is just down the street from Lee Circle, but there wasn't a clear or safe line of sight, so for the next couple of hours, my top staff moved a few blocks away to try to get a bird's-eye view of the statue coming down. We watched the local news, which had gone to near twenty-four-hour coverage of the removal, almost like they would in a hurricane. It was only when I learned from the police that the statue was gone and there had been no riot that I felt a certain sensation of stress melting away.

I felt a greater relief, but also sort of raw in the weeks and months that followed. I was hurt by the level of anger and hate that I thought we in New Orleans had finally put behind us. I can hear a few guys saying, *Well, Mitch, you led with your chin.* I had won reelection three years earlier with a resounding majority of white and black voters. My support in the black community stayed strong, but I'd lost nearly half of the white support, according to the polls, since taking on the monuments. The speech gave me a great deal of favorable attention in the national media; but in my hometown, the tide has not so quickly turned. I hope that in setting down my experiences and thoughts at length in this book that many of those who once stood against taking the monuments down will think again and commit to working through the issues of race in our country after learning more about our real history.

The long strain that Cheryl and I dealt with through this ordeal left us with a trailing sense of sadness, as we realized that people we thought shared our belief in racial harmony could not go that extra mile. But it also taught us about the possibilities of change, and a few lessons about not writing off people with whom you've clashed; they may surprise you yet. Another way of thinking of it might be that forgiveness is elemental to getting along in life as well as in politics.

I could blame Wynton Marsalis for putting me in this pickle, but the truth is, he dared me, as only a friend can do, to take a principled stand and do the just thing, no matter what the political fallout. I will always be thankful to him for it. Politics does not provide many moments for an elected official to take a moral stand, realizing that you may well pay a political price in doing so, but knowing in your heart you've done something that will make you a better human being.

Epilogue

Pope Paul VI in the 1960s declared: "If you want peace, work for justice." Today we hear his words with an altering twist: "Where there is no justice there is no peace." I heard a lot about justice and peace at marches and from activists, especially in the wake of Ferguson, Baltimore, and Baton Rouge. "No justice, no peace!" My entire life I thought that meant, "If you don't give me what is rightfully mine, I'm gonna hurt you, I'm gonna take it by any means necessary." I took it as an implied threat.

I didn't really get that what it actually meant was, if everything is not fair, it creates alienation. And when people are alienated from one another, and they can't share with one another what it is that they have, it is likely to lead to some level of violence. Poverty is a form of violence, I believe. So is not having access to health care, or not having a real job so that you, too, can create generational wealth for your family. There is an institutional violence, as Robert Kennedy told us many, many years ago, that comes with there not being any justice.

So where there is no justice, there can be no peace. A columnist for the New Orleans *Times-Picayune*, Jarvis DeBerry, put it more simply:

> The phrase "No justice, no peace" is probably as misunderstood and misconstrued as the phrase "Black lives matter." The same people who hear "Black lives matter" as indifference to other people's well-being are likely the same people who hear "No justice, no peace" as a promise to hurt somebody. If somebody said, "No rain, no flowers" or "No pain, no gain," the meaning would be clear: the second thing won't happen without the first. The speaker wouldn't be accused of spitefully keeping flowers from growing out of anger at a drought."

We all come to the table of democracy in the United States of America as equals. That's the aspiration. *That's* what makes America great. That is what everybody has a right to, that is what everybody is entitled to, but in order for you to get there, you have got to bring somebody along with you. This isn't what we merely aspire to; it is a truth that cannot be denied: that we are all better together, because we all benefit from one another. We all have to go forward together, or we don't go forward at all. Now, again, just like "no justice, no peace," that's not a threat. It's not a playground game, where if you don't give me what I want, you're not gonna get what you want, cause I'm not gonna give it to you. It's not a sacrifice, or a zero-sum game (if you win, I lose). It's an invitation for us to do better, together. To understand that we all benefit when we are truly at the table as equals. So, if you are the mayor of the city and you want to take a culture of violence and turn it into a culture of peace, you have to produce justice, because if there is no justice, there is no peace. I only understand that today because of what we faced. It shouldn't have to take that kind of ordeal for the rest of America to get it. But as this writing was coming to a close, another lawsuit was filed to invalidate the laws cited to enable our moving the statues. Even after the statues are down and even after what happened in Charlottesville, there are still folks fighting hard to revive the message of the Lost Cause.

As I think about how to move forward, I am reminded of the many teachers on race and equity that I have been blessed to meet and engage with in my role as mayor. Bryan Stevenson, Marian Wright Edelman, John Lewis, Barack Obama, Henry Louis Gates, Orlando Patterson, Cornel West, Charles Blow, Michael Eric Dyson, Ta-Nahesi Coates, Angela Glover Blackwell, Jesmyn Ward, Judy Reese Morse, and many others who have challenged me and fed my intellectual curiosity. I have benefited greatly from their work and, more important, their perspectives, even when I disagree (as I have sometimes). I will continue to be a lifelong learner on these topics, as this is one of the best ways to understand and grow as a human being.

I am often reminded of the lyrics of a song from one of my favorite shows, *South Pacific*, a brilliant musical in my view. I am still struck by the way Rodgers and Hammerstein handled the experiences of GIs on an island in the Second World War, a place where different cultures intersected and where we could see dramatized the yearning soldiers felt to finally go home. I was in high school when I saw the film version and played the record over and over. The song I'm thinking of is called "You've Got to Be Carefully Taught." The gist is that hate is a learned behavior, passed down from parents to children, generation after generation. Hate is not the natural order of things. The question then remains—what do we need to do to unlearn it?

I now realize that in those lyrics I was hearing a counter-story to my own life, as I remembered parents who carefully taught us to embrace people whose skin was a different shade, not to hate or fear "the other." The Jesuits stressed that we should be "men for others," a message that has been central to my life in politics.

During my work on this book, Will Landrieu, the youngest of our five, a basketball player at Jesuit, was filling out college applications, and showed me his entrance essay. With Will's permission, I share part of it here.

Growing up as the son of the mayor of New Orleans, I have seen the struggles of leadership. In response to years of discussion, my father decided to remove the Confederate monuments found across our city. He delivered a speech on the topic that though nationally applauded, was locally controversial. There was discord in the city leading to tense protests that bordered on violence. Despite thirty years of earning the public's approval, the vitriol thrust through my father's professional life directly to the daily lives of our family. We didn't feel safe anywhere or with anyone.

For the two days after the removal, I walked down the school hallway bracing myself as my classmates yelled out "nigger lover" and "your dad is ruining the city." My closest friends even sent me articles with false rumors about my father. Until now, I have kept these words to myself.

Standing up for others is excruciatingly lonely. I know my dad must be more hurt and lonely than I am. As my black friends explain, at least my family is lonely by choice. They were simply born just a little bit darker than I was. Until the monuments were removed, my friends never imagined they would live a day where they wouldn't walk the hallways, or sit in history class, in fear of the next hateful comment.

I know the decision is right because my friends would want someone to stand up for them. I have the ability to do that, so I intend to take full advantage of my privilege. I know that great decisions have great costs, but those costs are a fraction of what the people we are making them for have endured.

I will let paternal pride fall away and admit when I read Will's lines, I thought back to the woman berating me as an eighth grader outside the gym of that same school, and thought back to the phone calls on South Prieur Street when my dad was mayor and my mother took the calls, shielding us from the hostility of hateful anonymous voices. My son is correct in saying that there is a loneliness that comes with standing up for others; and yet I ultimately am proud of how far we have moved the conversation. If behavior is learned and passed on, that means we can continue to make progress, one person, one family at a time.

Politics in the highest sense is grounded in hope. If we put our best instincts and willing minds to the common good, we can rebuild what has been destroyed by storms, derailed by hate, or eroded by neglect, and steer our society on a saner, safer course. We can pass on the promise of America to our young. We have made great strides in that direction in this city I have been privileged to govern.

"I am sorry." "I forgive you." Perhaps the six most powerful words in the English language. Staying mad is no strategy for getting better or ahead or for feeding our families. We seem to spend a lot of time assigning blame to others. It's a never-ending search. I can't ever figure out whose fault anything is. But I am pretty clear that I have a responsibility to help fix whatever is broken. And so do you. As Father Tompson would say, go do the thing that will do the most good for the most people, in the shortest amount of time.

One of my great thrills as mayor is to know that NASA has chosen the Michoud Assembly Facility in New Orleans East to build the rocket that will eventually take a human mission to Mars. It's part of the Orion Mission. Those of us old enough to remember the excitement of watching Neil Armstrong set foot on the moon in 1969 know it was the culmination of our hopes for a soaring America, a show of our pioneering spirit, a determination to do really big things.

Rather than a look backward, space exploration is America's bold commitment to explore the world's new frontier. As impossible and daunting as it seems, we invest time, technology, know-how, grit, determination, money, aspiration, and dreams. We suffer setbacks and defeats. And yet we keep trying, never doubting our ability to find the outer reaches of the universe in a quest for knowledge that could improve the quality of our lives on earth.

When we testify in court, we swear to tell the truth, the whole truth, and nothing but the truth. This is important because anything but the whole truth and nothing but the truth will lead us astray. Unfortunately, that is the story of the American history most of us know, particularly as it relates to race. To move forward, we must commit to tell the whole truth about our past. To move forward, we must find that new space on race here, a zone of belief that holds promise for a nation committed to justice for all of our people, making right what we have failed to do, and insisting that we will do what it takes to reach the next threshold for humankind. We find that new space, in politics and society, if we confirm our belief in democracy as a welcome table for people created equal under God, where the pursuit of equity is an open field for opportunity and responsibility. As the scientists continually course-correct a mission error in order to make the next flight safer, so we must learn to revise the mistakes in our perceptions of history, to acknowledge with honesty what went wrong so that we can learn how to make it right. We are all being called to a better day, a better South, a better America. I have great faith that we will respond well to that call. Now is the time to choose our path forward.

A few friends who have written books before cautioned me that the hardest part about writing a book is the acknowledgments, because someone indispensable will undoubtedly be left off. So let me start by thanking all of you for reading this book and giving me an opportunity to share my thoughts on history and this moment we find ourselves in today.

This work is the culmination of nearly thirty years of public service to the people of Louisiana. Throughout it all, I have sought to fight for justice, and perhaps more relevant today, to fight for truth. It's been both an honor and a burden. The honor comes from the incredible opportunity to be in the middle of this awesome thing we call democracy, in good times and in bad, which leads us—sometimes lurches us—forward, sometimes backward, and hopefully at last toward a better nation. The burden, honestly, comes from the intense isolation and loneliness one feels and the weight of being responsible for the safety, security, and well-being of the people you have been entrusted to serve. It is a burden that I chose to bear and one that I would gladly do again. But it is a burden nonetheless, and it has hurt pretty badly from time to time. At the end of the day, the joy outweighed the pain and the sacrifice was worth it. After thirty years of stellar service to the people of my state, most people will only ever remember that I took down some statues. If I had my wish, they would say that I helped rebuild a broken city and took a huge step forward towards healing a hurting nation. But most importantly, that I was honest and sought the truth.

I'm not the only leader who has borne the honor and the burden of this work. I must also recognize the countless civil rights advocates, elected officials, and groups like Take 'Em Down NOLA in New Orleans and across the country that have also paved the way on issues of race and have done their part to bend the arc of the moral universe toward justice.

I can't remember doing or accomplishing anything by myself my entire life. Everything I have done well has been with the aid, assistance, and support of so many people. This book, of course, is no different.

To the people of New Orleans, I am indebted for the opportunity to serve the city I love so dearly. I pray that one day you realize how very special you are, and that you don't wait for the next catastrophe to begin to rise above small things, so you can get to the big stuff soon. You deserve it. To my fellow mayors across America, keep fighting the good fight. Thank you for inspiring me daily with your bold leadership.

I am grateful to the folks at Viking Penguin for guiding me through the process and for giving me the opportunity to share my thoughts with all of you. Thanks to the best editor you could ask for in Wendy Wolf, another New Orleans native, might I add. From the moment we first spoke, I knew she would ensure that this was a story grounded in speaking truth to power, but also truth in love—for as much as there is despair, from our hometown there is a message of hope, resurrection, and redemption. To my agents, Keith Urbahn, Matt Latimer, and the team at Javelin, your counsel and advice throughout has been invaluable.

This process has been easy because of the great talents of New Orleans's own Jason Berry. Jason, of course, achieved prominence for his investigative reporting on the Catholic Church abuse crisis in the 1990s. I first got to know him well while he was exposing David Duke in the 1980s and '90s; he has been everything you could ask for in a collaborator. I know this was a heavy lift for him as he carved out time from work on his forthcoming history of New Orleans, *City of a Million Dreams*, to assist me, nights and weekends, given my daily schedule. I am eternally grateful for his time, talent, and friendship throughout this writing process.

Those who have worked with me know that I go through dozens of versions of a speech before I give it. Sam Joel has been my scribe and speechwriter over the past eight years.

This book and most speeches would not have been possible without the shepherding and writing of Ryan Berni from beginning to end.

To my staff at City Hall, literally the best team in America: I can do what I do because you dedicate your life to a cause greater than one's self. You are the team who helped rebuild a broken city, who reengineered an improbable comeback story. As if that weren't enough, you endured the grueling work through trying times in the attempt to get the statues down. There were protests. There were threats. But through it all, you not only kept your eyes focused on the end, you also kept the city running well, laying a stronger foundation for the future. Thank you, thank you, thank you, Brooke Smith, Judy Reese Morse, Ryan Berni, Rebecca Dietz, Jeff Hebert, Cedric Grant, Scott Hutcheson, Sam Joel, Tyronne Walker, Sarah Robertson Miller, Zach Butterworth, Aaron Miller, Vincent Smith, Dani Galloway, Katie Dignan, Michael Harrison, Timmy McConnell, George Patterson, Eddie Sens, Andy Kopplin, Emily Arata, Sharonda Williams, Alex Lebow, Suzie Sepcich, April Davenport, Glenda Patterson, Mary Pettingill, Erin Burns, Bob, Gary, and many others. And to all of their families, who sacrificed so much of their time during our service together.

Thanks to Flozell Daniels and the Foundation for Louisiana for stepping up to serve as a fiscal partner in the monument removal effort. And to all the philanthropic donors who assisted.

To Ruth and Larry Kullman and Norma Jane Sabiston, whose friendship and guidance I rely upon daily. Thanks also to Scott Shalett.

I will always be indebted to the spiritual guidance and moral clarity of two Jesuit priests, Father Harry Tompson and Father Paul Schott, and finally to the Men of Manresa for keeping me in your prayers. AMDG.

To my eight brothers and sisters, thank you for your friendship, love, and support.

A special thanks and note of gratitude to my father and mother, Moon and Verna Landrieu. As a young boy, I watched my father help integrate our great American city. His strength, his resolve, his clarity of vision, and his relentless focus on the people he served inspires me every day. My mother, keeping all nine of us kids in check while also serving as my dad's most important adviser, is the closest living person to a saint. They taught all nine of us to love one another. To be fair, honest, and just. They taught us to work hard and play hard. To be thankful and to help others. You are my heroes and role models.

As it should be, my unconditional love and thanks to my wife, Cheryl, and our five kids, Grace, Emily, Matt, Ben, and Will. Thank you for your sacrifices. I love you.

And finally, to one of my heroes, John Lewis, who gives me the courage to keep going and to stand in the face of danger even when you know you are going to get hit.

FURTHER READING

Among the many books on New Orleans and Louisiana that I
have read over the years, these were particularly helpful in the
work on *In the Shadow of Statues*.

Tyler Bridges, *The Rise of David Duke* (Jackson: University Press of
Mississippi, 1994)

Freddi Williams Evans, *Congo Square: African Roots in New Orleans*
(Lafayette, LA: ULL Press, 2011)

Jed Horne, *Breach of Faith: Hurricane Katrina and the Near Death of a
Great American City* (New York: Random House, 2006)

Sybil Kein, ed., *Creole: The History and Legacy of Louisiana's Free People
of Color* (Baton Rouge: Louisiana State University Press, 2000)

James W. Loewen, *Lies Across America: What Our Historic Sites Get
Wrong* (New York: Touchstone, 2000)

James W. Loewen and Edward H. Sebesta, *The Confederate and
Neo-Confederate Reader: The "Great Truth" about the "Lost Cause"*
(Jackson: University Press of Mississippi, 2010)

Keith Weldon Medley, *Black Life in Old New Orleans* (Gretna, LA:
Pelican Publishing, 2014)

Lawrence N. Powell, *The Accidental City: Improvising New Orleans*
(Cambridge, MA: Harvard University Press, 2012)

Douglas D. Rose, ed., *The Emergence of David Duke and the Politics of
Race* (Chapel Hill: University of North Carolina Press, 1992)

Ibrahima Seck, *Bouki Fait Gombo: A History of the Slave Community of
Habitation Haydel (Whitney Plantation), Louisiana, 1750–1860* (New
Orleans, LA: UNO Press, 2014)

Jesmyn Ward, *Salvage the Bones* (New York: Bloomsbury, 2011)

TRUTH: REMARKS ON THE REMOVAL OF CONFEDERATE MONUMENTS IN NEW ORLEANS

Gallier Hall
Friday, May 19, 2017

Text from the Speech

Thank you for coming.

The soul of our beloved city is deeply rooted in a history that has evolved over thousands of years; rooted in a diverse people who have been here together every step of the way—for both good and for ill.

It is a history that holds in its heart the stories of Native Americans—the Choctaw, Houma Nation, the Chitimacha.

Of Hernando de Soto, Robert Cavelier, Sieur de La Salle, the Acadians, the Isleños, the enslaved people from Senegambia, Free People of Color, the Haitians, the Germans, both the empires of France and Spain. The Italians, the Irish, the Cubans, the South and Central Americans, the Vietnamese and so many more.

You see—New Orleans is truly a city of many nations, a melting pot, a bubbling cauldron of many cultures.

There is no other place quite like it in the world that so

eloquently exemplifies the uniquely American motto: *e pluribus unum*—out of many we are one.

But there are also other truths about our city that we must confront.

New Orleans was America's largest slave market: a port where hundreds of thousands of souls were brought, sold, and shipped up the Mississippi River to lives of forced labor, of misery, of rape, of torture.

America was the place where nearly 4,000 of our fellow citizens were lynched, 540 alone in Louisiana; where the courts enshrined "separate but equal"; where Freedom Riders coming to New Orleans were beaten to a bloody pulp.

So when people say to me that the monuments in question are history, well, what I just described is real history as well, and it is the searing truth.

And it immediately begs the questions; why there are no slave ship monuments, no prominent markers on public land to remember the lynchings or the slave blocks; nothing to remember this long chapter of our lives; the pain, the sacrifice, the shame . . . all of it happening on the soil of New Orleans.

So for those self-appointed defenders of history and the monuments, they are eerily silent on what amounts to this historical malfeasance, a lie by omission.

There is a difference between remembrance of history and reverence of it.

For America and New Orleans, it has been a long, winding road, marked by great tragedy and great triumph. But we cannot be afraid of our truth.

As President George W. Bush said at the dedication ceremony for the National Museum of African American History and Culture, "A great nation does not hide its history. It faces its flaws and corrects them."

So today I want to speak about why we chose to remove these four monuments to the Lost Cause of the Confederacy, but also how and why this process can move us toward healing and understanding of each other.

So, let's start with the facts.

The historic record is clear, the Robert E. Lee, Jefferson Davis, and P. G. T. Beauregard statues were *not* erected just to honor these men, but as part of the movement that became known as the Cult of the Lost Cause.

This "cult" had one goal—through monuments and through other means—to rewrite history to hide the truth, which is that the Confederacy was on the wrong side of humanity.

First erected over 166 years *after* the founding of our city and 19 years *after* the end of the Civil War, the monuments that we took down were meant to rebrand the history of our city and the ideals of a defeated Confederacy.

It is self-evident that these men did not fight for the United States of America, they fought against it. They may have been warriors, but in this cause they were not patriots.

These statues are not just stone and metal. They are not just innocent remembrances of a benign history.

These monuments purposefully celebrate a fictional, sanitized Confederacy; ignoring the death, ignoring the enslavement, and the terror that it actually stood for.

After the Civil War, these statues were a part of that terrorism as much as a burning cross on someone's lawn; they were erected purposefully to send a strong message to all who walked in their shadows about who was still in charge in this city.

Should you have further doubt about the true goals of the Confederacy, in the very weeks before the war broke out, the vice president of the Confederacy Alexander Stephens made it clear that the Confederate cause was about maintaining slavery and white supremacy.

He said in his now famous "corner-stone speech" that the Confederacy's "*corner-stone rests upon the great truth, that the negro is not equal to the white man; that slavery—subordination to the superior race—is his natural and normal condition. This, our new government, is the first, in the history of the world, based upon this great physical, philosophical, and moral truth.*"

Now, with these shocking words still ringing in your ears . . .

I want to try to gently peel from your hands the grip on a false narrative of our history that I think weakens us, and make straight a wrong turn we made many years ago—so we can more closely connect with integrity to the founding principles of our nation and forge a clearer and straighter path toward a better city and a more perfect union.

Last year, President Barack Obama echoed these sentiments about the need to contextualize and remember *all* our history.

He recalled a piece of stone, a slave auction block engraved with a marker commemorating a single moment in 1830 when Andrew Jackson and Henry Clay stood and spoke from it.

President Obama said, "Consider what this artifact tells us about history . . . on a stone where day after day for years, men and women . . . bound and bought and sold and bid like cattle on a stone worn down by the tragedy of over a thousand bare feet. For a long time the only thing we considered important, the singular thing we once chose to commemorate as history with a plaque were the unmemorable speeches of two powerful men."

A piece of stone—one stone.

Both stories were history.

One story told.

One story forgotten or maybe even purposefully ignored.

As clear as it is for me today . . . for a long time, even though I grew up in one of New Orleans's most diverse neighborhoods, even with my family's long, proud history of fighting for civil rights . . . I must have passed by those monuments a million times without giving them a second thought.

So I am not judging anybody, I am not judging people. We all take our own journey on race. I just hope people listen like I did when my dear friend Wynton Marsalis helped me see the truth.

He asked me to think about all the people who have left New Orleans because of our exclusionary attitudes.

Another friend asked me to consider these four monuments from the perspective of an African American mother or father trying to explain to their fifth-grade daughter who Robert E. Lee is and why he stands atop of our beautiful city.

Can you do it?

Can you look into that young girl's eyes and convince her that Robert E. Lee is there to encourage her? Do you think she will feel inspired and hopeful by that story?

Do these monuments help her see a future with limitless potential? Have you ever thought that if her potential is limited, yours and mine are, too?

We all know the answer to these very simple questions.

When you look into this child's eyes is the moment when

the searing truth comes into focus for us. This is the moment when we know what is right and what we must do.

We can't walk away from this truth.

And I knew that taking down the monuments was going to be tough, but you elected me to do the right thing, not the easy thing, and this is what that looks like.

So relocating these Confederate monuments is *not* about taking something away from someone else. This is *not* about politics, this is not about blame or retaliation.

This is *not* a naïve quest to solve all our problems at once.

This is, however, about showing the whole world that we as a city and as a people are able to acknowledge, understand, reconcile, and most importantly, choose a better future for ourselves, making straight what has been crooked and making right what was wrong.

Otherwise, we will continue to pay a price with discord, with division, and yes, with violence.

To literally put the Confederacy on a pedestal in our most prominent places of honor is an inaccurate recitation of our full past, it is an affront to our present, and it is a bad prescription for our future.

History cannot be changed. It cannot be moved like a statue. What is done is done. The Civil War is over, and the Confederacy lost and we are better for it.

Surely we are far enough removed from this dark time to acknowledge that the cause of the Confederacy was wrong.

And in the second decade of the twenty-first century, asking African Americans—or anyone else—to drive by property that *they own* occupied by reverential statues of men who fought to destroy the country and deny that person's humanity seems perverse and absurd.

Centuries-old wounds are still raw because they never healed right in the first place.

Here is the essential truth: We are better together than we are apart.

Indivisibility is our essence.

Isn't this the gift that the people of New Orleans have given to the world?

We radiate beauty and grace in our food, in our music, in our architecture, in our joy of life, in our celebration of death; in everything that we do.

We gave the world this funky thing called jazz, the most uniquely American art form that is developed across the ages from different cultures.

Think about second lines, think about Mardi Gras, think about muffaletta, think about the Saints, gumbo, red beans and rice.

By God, just think.

All we hold dear is created by throwing everything in the pot; creating, producing something better; everything a product of our historic diversity.

We are proof that out of many we are one—and better for it! Out of many we are one—and we really do love it!

And yet, we still seem to find so many excuses for not doing the right thing. Again, remember President Bush's words, "A great nation does not hide its history. It faces its flaws and corrects them."

We forget, we deny how much we really depend on each other, how much we need each other.

We justify our silence and inaction by manufacturing noble causes that marinate in historical denial.

We still find a way to say "wait," not so fast, but like

Dr. Martin Luther King, Jr., said, "Wait has almost always meant never."

We can't wait any longer. We need to change. And we need to change now. No more waiting. This is not just about statues, this is about our attitudes and behavior as well.

If we take these statues down and don't change to become a more open and inclusive society this would have all been in vain.

While some have driven by these monuments every day and either revered their beauty or failed to see them at all, many of our neighbors and fellow Americans see them very clearly.

Many are painfully aware of the long shadows their presence casts; not only literally but figuratively.

And they clearly receive the message that the Confederacy and the Cult of the Lost Cause intended to deliver.

Earlier this week, as the Cult of the Lost Cause statue of P. G. T Beauregard came down, world-renowned musician Terence Blanchard stood watch, his wife, Robin, and their two beautiful daughters at their side.

Terence went to a high school on the edge of City Park named after one of America's greatest heroes and patriots, John F. Kennedy.

But to get there he had to pass by this monument to a man who fought to deny him his humanity.

He said, "I've never looked at them as a source of pride . . . it's always made me feel as if they were put there by people who don't respect us.

"This is something I never thought I'd see in my lifetime. It's a sign that the world is changing."

Yes, Terence, it is and it is long overdue.

Now is the time to send a new message to the next

generation of New Orleanians who can follow in Terence and Robin's remarkable footsteps.

A message about the future, about the next three hundred years and beyond; let us not miss this opportunity, New Orleans, and let us help the rest of the country do the same.

Because now is the time for choosing.

Now is the time to actually make this the city we always should have been, had we gotten it right in the first place.

We should stop for a moment and ask ourselves—at this point in our history—after Katrina, after Rita, after Ike, after Gustav, after the national recession, after the BP oil catastrophe, and after the tornado—if presented with the opportunity to build monuments that told our story or to curate these particular spaces . . . would these monuments be what we want the world to see? Is this really our story?

We have not erased history; we are becoming part of the city's history by righting the wrong image these monuments represent and crafting a better, more complete future for all our children and for future generations.

And unlike when these Confederate monuments were first erected as symbols of white supremacy, we now have a chance to create not only new symbols, but to do it together, as one people.

In our blessed land we *all* come to the table of democracy as equals.

We have to reaffirm our commitment to a future where each citizen is guaranteed the uniquely American gifts of life, liberty, and the pursuit of happiness.

That is what really makes America great, and today it is more important than ever to hold fast to these values and together say a self-evident truth that out of many we are one.

That is why today we reclaim these spaces for the United States of America.

Because we are *one* nation, not two; indivisible with liberty and justice for all . . . not some.

We all are part of one nation, all pledging allegiance to one flag, the flag of the United States of America.

And New Orleanians are in . . . all of the way.

It is in this union and in this truth that real patriotism is rooted and flourishes.

Instead of revering a four-year, brief historical aberration that was called the Confederacy, we can celebrate all three hundred years of our rich, diverse history as a place named New Orleans, and set the tone for the *next* three hundred years.

After decades of public debate, of anger, of anxiety, of anticipation, of humiliation, and of frustration.

After public hearings and approvals from three separate community-led commissions.

After two robust public hearings and a 6–1 vote by the duly elected New Orleans City Council.

After review by thirteen different federal and state judges.

The full weight of the legislative, executive, and judicial branches of government has been brought to bear and the monuments in accordance with the law have been removed.

So now is the time to come together and heal and focus on our larger task. Not only building new symbols, but making this city a beautiful manifestation of what is possible and what we as a people can become.

Let us remember what the once exiled, imprisoned, and now universally loved Nelson Mandela said after the fall of apartheid.

"If the pain has often been unbearable and the revelations

shocking to all of us, it is because they indeed bring us the beginnings of a common understanding of what happened and a steady restoration of the nation's humanity."

So before we part let us again state the truth clearly.

The Confederacy was on the wrong side of history and humanity. It sought to tear apart our nation and subjugate our fellow Americans to slavery. This is the history we should never forget and one that we should never again put on a pedestal to be revered.

As a community, we must recognize the significance of removing New Orleans's Confederate monuments.

It is our acknowledgment that now is the time to take stock of, and then move past, a painful part of our history.

Anything less would render generations of courageous struggle and soul-searching a truly lost cause.

Anything less would fall short of the immortal words of our greatest president, Abraham Lincoln, who with an open heart and clarity of purpose called on us today to unite as one people when he said:

"With malice toward none, with charity for all, with firmness in the right as God gives us to see the right, let us strive on to finish the work we are in, to bind up the nation's wounds . . . to do *all* which may achieve *and* cherish a just and lasting peace among ourselves and with all nations."

Thank you.